Alexander Tulloch

WORD ROUTES

JOURNEYS THROUGH ETYMOLOGY

Peter Owen
London and Chester Springs

PETER OWEN PUBLISHERS
73 Kenway Road, London SW5 0RE

Peter Owen books are distributed in the USA by
Dufour Editions Inc., Chester Springs, PA 19425-0007

ISBN 0 7206 1243 8

Printed in Great Britain by
Bookmarque Ltd

contents

introduction

The title of this volume was chosen deliberately. There are many, many books available to the amateur and professional linguist on the roots of English. By and large such works tend to concentrate on historically linear derivations and seldom explore the way in which English words relate to others in other languages. My aim is to demonstrate how the words we use every day have frequently travelled not just down through time from a parent language but outwards across continents as well. To this end, my first priority has been to lead the reader, as far as possible, from the historical *root* of a word to its present form, showing the *route* it has taken and the connections it has forged with other related languages during its progress into English.

In the nature of things this has meant that some entries are much fuller than others. Some words have altered little over the centuries and have forged few, if any, links with others but are none the less interesting etymologically and have therefore been included here. Other words have spread their influence through history like giant tentacles, twisting and turning in the process, with the result that words in languages as far apart in time and geographical location as Ancient Greek or Sanskrit can show up in the modern forms of Irish Gaelic, Russian or English – but often with quite dramatic changes of meaning. Who would suspect, for instance, that the word 'champion' is linguistically related to the Ancient Greek word for a bend in a river? Or, as we listen to the carol singers at Christmas, who among us would make the etymological connection between these festive hymns and the Russian for a beehive? And who would believe, without adequate proof, that the tall vigorous trees surrounding us on a Sunday afternoon stroll in the woods were such a powerful symbol of strength to our forebears that they have given us our word 'endure' and the Russians their word for health?

In putting this volume together my *modus operandi* has been quite simple and straightforward. I have unashamedly plundered authoritative etymological foreign and English dictionaries and any other sources that seemed appropriate. Generally speaking I have taken one word in an English etymological dictionary (Skeat, Wyld, etc.) and then followed its path wherever it led through foreign etymological and non-etymological dictionaries. Of particular use and help here have been Liddel and Scott's *Greek–English Lexicon* and *The Historical and Etymological Dictionary of the Russian Language* by P. Ya. Chernykh.

In cases where there has been a difference of opinion between established authorities I have usually sided with neither but merely mentioned the various theories and left the reader to choose. On other occasions I have consulted works of a similar nature in a effort to point the reader in the direction of what is most likely to be the correct interpretation of the available evidence. In such cases John Ayto's *Dictionary of Word Origins* has been particularly useful.

I have has also preferred to confine myself to safe territory and deal with those languages with which I am most familiar. Only rarely have I ventured beyond the borders of familiarity, and consequently French, Spanish, German, Russian, Greek and Irish Gaelic feature prominently in the text, whereas Portuguese, Italian, Hindi and many other important Indo-European languages are not often mentioned.

Most of what we think of today as European languages fall into the group referred to by linguists as Indo-European (also known in older texts as Aryan). Broadly speaking, this group, as the name suggests, covers the languages of Europe and northern India and a number of languages in between – notably Persian, Kurdish and languages in Afghanistan – and further subdivides into several main categories: Indo-Iranian (Hindi, Bengali and other languages of northern India, as well as Persian); Baltic (Latvian, Lithuanian but not Estonian); Slavonic (Russian, Bulgarian, Polish, Czech, etc.); Germanic (Scandinavian languages, German, English); Romance (Latin, French, Spanish, Italian, etc.); Hellenic (Greek); and Celtic (Irish and Scots Gaelic, Welsh, Breton, Manx and Cornish).

Languages such as Albanian and Armenian each form individual branches of Indo-European with virtually no known affinity to any other language group.

Not all the modern languages of Europe are Indo-European, however, and there are some anomalies. Languages such as Hungarian and Finnish, for example, are geographically European but linguistically unrelated to the Indo-European group. And Basque, a complex and ancient language spoken by some 700,000 people in an area of northern Spain and southern France, also falls outside the Indo-European group and is apparently unrelated to any other language anywhere in the world.

It is very difficult to date the appearance of the Indo-European family of languages with absolute certainty, but there seems to be little disagreement among etymologists that they existed well before 2000 BC. It is only relatively recently that people have begun to take an interest in the evolution of languages on the continental land mass, and it all started when Sir William Jones, probably the first etymologist, pointed out the great similarity between Sanskrit, the ancient language of the Hindus of India, and Latin and Greek. This is not the place for a detailed exposition of these similarities, but the reader might find it of interest to compare a few of the numerals in these languages as an indicator of the affinity they bear with each other:

Sanskrit	Ancient Greek	Latin
eka	heis	unus
dvi	duo	duo
tri	treis	tres
catur	tessares	quattuor
panca	pente	quinque
sas	hex	sex
sapta	hepta	septem
asta	okto	octo
nava	ennea	novem
dasa	deka	decem

To the uninitiated the similarities in all may not seem apparent. There is the obvious linguistic affinity between all three languages for two and three, for example, but that between other numerals may not seem as convincing until we consider the phenomenon known as the 'sound shifts'.

Language is organic. It never stands still, and what was a current word or expression yesterday might today be considered *passé* and tomorrow be completely forgotten. This applies not only to words, expressions and what generally might be referred as vocabulary but also the sounds of a particular language. Such changes can and do also take place as words make their way from one language or one language group to another. The reader of this volume will frequently come across references to Indo-European interchanges which explain why the same word can appear in different languages in what might appear to be totally unrelated forms.

It was Jacob Grimm who, in 1822, published what has now come to be known as 'Grimm's Law'. This was an attempt to categorize the changes that had taken place over the centuries as words move from one Indo-European language to another. He noticed, for example, that the letter 'p' in Sanskrit, Latin or Greek almost always produced the sound 'f' when the word moved into the Germanic languages, referred to throughout as the p/f interchange. Hence the English 'father' and German *Vater* but Sanskrit *pitar*, Greek *patēr* and Latin *pater*. It also explains why Sanskrit and Greek have *panca* and *pente* where English and German have 'five' and *fünf*.

A similar pattern emerges if we consider the letter 's'. Where this sound occurred in Sanskrit it appeared with an aspirate 'h' sound in Greek but retained its original sound in all the other Indo-European language groups (the h/s interchange). Hence the English word 'serpent' is related to the Sanskrit *sarpas* and its Latin equivalent *serpens* and also to the Greek verb *herpō*, to creep (and the medical condition 'herpes', because of its characteristic creeping progression over the skin). This sound shift also explains why English has 'six' and 'seven' but the equivalent numbers in Greek are *hex* and *hepta*.

Another phenomenon noted by the earlier philologists was that words in one language denoting family relationships frequently bore a close resemblance to the equivalent terms in other languages of the same group. We have already mentioned 'father', and even the most cursory glance at other words defining relationships illustrates a similar linguistic affinity. English 'mother' has its counterparts in French *mère,* Spanish *madre,* Russian *mat',* Latin *mater* and Greek *metēr.* And the Sanskrit for brother, *bhrata,* is obviously related to our word 'brother', the Russian *brat,* German *Bruder,* Latin *frater* and French *frère.* (Modern Irish has the cognate *brathair,* although this is 'brother' in the ecclesiastical sense rather than a term defining close family relationship.)

Anyone who opens these pages will be struck almost immediately with the frequent references made to Latin and Ancient Greek. The reason for this is obvious. No study of the history of English (or any other Indo-European language for that matter) can be complete without constant reference to these so-called 'dead' languages. Once again, this is not the place for a prolix exegesis of the academically suicidal error committed by those who decided to dispense with teaching these languages in our schools and universities, but a passing observation is permissible. The classical languages have played, and still play, such an important role in the development of our own language that any explanation of the derivation of English words will, by its very nature, include frequent reference to them. Many words we use in everyday language ('video', 'doctor', 'television', 'centre', 'language', 'school', etc.) have come from Latin or Greek directly into English. And let us not forget that these languages are much, much older than English and cannot be ignored if linguistic history is to be studied at any meaningful depth. Greek, for instance, is the European language with the longest unbroken history, as it has written records which can be traced back as far as 700 BC.

The Greek and Latin verbs the reader will encounter in this book require a special mention. When a Greek verb is quoted here it is generally in the first person singular form, even though the English equivalent given is the infinitive. Thus, under 'AFTERMATH',

11

amaō is given as 'to reap' when, strictly speaking, it should be 'I reap'. The reasons for this approach are straightforward. In the first place, I am merely obeying the standard convention employed in most dictionaries and, in the second, the Greek verbal system is such that a verb can have up to nine infinitives, whereas there is normally only one form of the first person of the present tense.

With Latin verbs I have also chosen to stay with convention and give the four principal parts wherever appropriate. Thus, under 'OBITUARY', parts of the quoted Latin verb are first person singular *obeo* (I go down), the infinitive *obire* (to go down), the first person perfect tense *obivi* (I have gone down) and the supine, a verbal adjective used under certain circumstances to replace the infinitive proper. It is also the part of the verb from which the past participle passive of a transitive verb is formed. Where the verb is entirely regular in the formation of its principal parts (e.g. *amo, amare, amavi, amatum*), only the first person and/or the infinitive have been quoted.

I would like to claim that this tome represents a highly original work of scholarship. Unfortunately this would be somewhat misleading, as the only claim to originality I can make is in the manner of the presentation. All the information contained here has been available for decades in dictionaries of one sort or another, and I have merely collated it and presented it in a form which perhaps has not been attempted before. I hope, however, that by concentrating on the paths words have taken from their historical origins (as far as this is possible) I will have produced a volume which can be read for fascination and interest as well as for instruction.

Alexander R. Tulloch

a

ABACUS

A wooden frame with movable beads still in use in parts of the world today for doing arithmetical calculations. The word has come into English from the Greek *abaks*, which was the term for a square-shaped board covered in sand in which the numbers were drawn with the finger. The Greek word was a borrowing from the Hebrew *abaq*, 'dust'.

ABSTEMIOUS

Now used to describe somebody who is generally not self-indulgent, but the original Latin word *abstemius*, from which it is derived, meant specifically 'not partaking of strong drink'. The component parts of the Latin word were *abs*, 'away from', and *temetum*, a word which could be applied to any strong drink and which is derived from the Indo-European root TAM, meaning 'to choke', 'to stifle'. The connection is probably the initial feeling of being gripped by the throat experienced with the first sip of spirits.

ACRE

Now a measure of land, this word has come down to us from Latin, Greek and Sanskrit (*ager*, *agros* and *ajra* respectively, all meaning 'field') and originally designated land reserved for hunting. This can be seen in the Indo-European root AK, 'to drive', 'to urge'. Another word linked to it linguistically is thought to be 'acorn', which originally meant 'fruit of the field'.

ACROBAT

From the Greek *akrobatēs*, literally meaning 'one who walks on tiptoe'. The first part of the word, *acro*, is from *akron*, 'the highest point' or 'the peak' of a mountain, and is the same word which is seen in the word *akropolis*, or, as we now write it, Acropolis, the 'high town' or citadel, especially that of Athens. The second element, *bat*, is from the Greek *batēs*, an inflection the verb *bainō*, 'to walk', 'to go'.

The Indo-European root is here AK, 'to pierce', a root that frequently appears in English and related languages in association with sharpness and pointed objects, etc. Take, for example, the expression 'to egg on'. This has nothing to do with shells in which oviparous creatures are born but is from the Anglo-Saxon *eggian*, 'to incite' or, more literally, 'to prick', 'to spur on'. The associated noun was *ecg*, meaning 'a sharp point' but which developed into modern English 'edge' with its inherent idea of sharpness, whether applied to a cliff face or a piece of everyday furniture.

Another related Greek verb, *agnumi*, 'to break', 'to snap', 'to crush', produced the noun *aksinē*, a tool for breaking up or chopping objects, which became our word 'axe'. And obviously an *aksinē* is more likely to chop, slice or cut efficiently if it is *oksus* or 'sharp'. When applied to food and drink this same adjective meant 'bitter' or 'acidic', and shows up also in the noun 'oxygen', the literal meaning of which is 'that which generates acid' as the gas was formerly believed to be essential in the formation of all acids. *Oksus* also found its way into Russian as *úksus*, 'vinegar'.

There is a further etymological link here with the word 'oxymoron', a literary term based on the juxtaposition of opposites such as 'bitter-sweet', 'a love–hate relationship' and 'cheerfully pessimistic'. The word itself is an oxymoron, being a combination of the adjectives *oksus* and *mōros*, 'sharp' and 'stupid'.

We have seen how the Greek noun *akron* designates the sharp peak or top of anything. Metaphorically, of course, the 'top' is associated with excellence. We can say that someone is 'the tops' or that someone is 'on top form' and talk about 'hitting the heights' when we mean that some venture has been very successful. On the other hand, if we decide that someone's talents are only 'mediocre' what we are really saying is that their talents are only sufficient to take them 'halfway up the hill'. The reasoning here is that the word 'mediocre' is from the Latin *mediocris*, 'ordinary', which is derived from *medius*, 'middle', and Old Latin (that is, prior to 75 BC) *acris*, 'peak', which is cognate with the Greek word *akron*.

AFTERMATH

Now used to mean 'the result or consequence of', but originally the word referred to the new crop of grass that began to grow after a field had been mown. The third syllable is derived from the Anglo-Saxon *mawan*, 'to mow', from an earlier Germanic root *mae*. The Anglo-Saxon origin of this word can be traced back to the Greek verb *amaō*, 'to reap', and is also cognate with the word 'meadow', the real meaning of which is a field in which the grass is mown for the purpose of providing hay. It also appears in Swiss place-names with the suffix *-matt*, such as Zermatt and Andermatt.

AKIMBO

To stand with one's arms akimbo is to stand with hands on hips, thus forming an angle at the elbow. The word is a contraction of the Old Norse in *kene bow*, 'in a sharp curve'. The word *kene* developed into modern English 'keen'.

AMBULANCE

We now think of an ambulance as a well-equipped vehicle which comes to our aid if we are suddenly taken ill or involved in an accident and require immediate medical treatment. The original ambulances, however, were somewhat different. From the Latin infinitive *ambulare*, 'to walk about', the first ones were nothing more than tents which served as crude field hospitals and could be moved rapidly from one part of the battlefield to another as the fortunes of war ebbed and flowed.

The original Latin verb has permeated into other languages, but in some cases the transition has involved a change of meaning. Spanish has the word *ambulancia*, which is both an 'ambulance' and a 'field hospital' in military parlance. But the noun derived from it, *ambulatorio*, is what in Britain would be referred to as a 'clinic'. Russian has *ambulatoriya* as the equivalent of what in Britain would be called an 'outpatients' department' or a GP's 'surgery'. In an emergency, however, a Muscovite would pick up the phone and call for a *mashina skoroy pomoshchi* or 'rapid assistance vehicle'.

Another word which is directly related linguistically to 'ambulance' in English is the verb 'to amble'. This word entered the language from Old French *ambler* in the fourteenth century, although at that time it was applied only to horses.

ANATHEMA

The evolution of this word is an excellent example of how words can sometimes change their meaning to such an extent that they end up meaning virtually the opposite of the original.

The Greek word *anathema* literally meant 'an offering up', from *ana*, 'up', and *tithēmi*, 'to put'. In Homer's time the word was used simply to denote an ornament – something which had be 'set up' to command the admiration of those who saw it. In Classical Greece the word was used to describe an offering or gift offered up to assuage a god. With the advent of Christianity and its intolerance of graven images and the like the word, because of its association with pagan traditions, gradually came to mean 'a curse'.

ANATOMY

Since the fourteenth century this word has been used to denote the scientific study of how the human body is structured. What tends to be forgotten is that before any study of a corpse can be made it has to be dissected or cut up. And this takes us, linguistically speaking, back to the Greeks, who had the words *ana*, 'up', and *temnō*, 'to cut', which combined to form the compound verb *anatemnō*, 'to cut up'.

Another Greek word derived from this verb was *tomos*, literally 'something cut out', which gave us the word 'tome', now virtually synonymous with 'book' or 'volume' but originally something which had been 'cut'. And the Latin for something which has been cut out is *sectio*, appearing in English as 'section'. The basic verb here is *seco, secare, secui, sectum,* which has spawned a host of words now in common use in English : 'sect' (cut off from a mainstream religion), 'secateurs' (borrowed from Latin through French, garden scissors) 'sector' (an area of land considered in isolation), to name but a few.

Perhaps not quite so obviously connected is the hairstyle traditionally associated with monks, the tonsure. The Greek verb *temnō* produced a variation *tendō*, meaning 'to gnaw at', 'to nibble at', and this passed into Latin as *tondeo, tondere, totondi, tonsum*, where it acquired the meaning 'to clip' or 'to shear'. The noun derived from it, *tonsura*, 'clipping', 'shaving', 'shearing', developed into 'tonsure'.

'That which cannot be cut' in Greek is expressed by the single word *atomos*, also derived from *temnō*, and this has given us the scientific name for the particle which is so small that it cannot be further divided, that is the 'atom'. And *atomo* in Modern Greek means 'a person' or 'an individual', someone who cannot be divided.

ANGER

The idea of uncontrollable wrath which we now link with this word was a relatively late development. Until the fourteenth century it meant 'grief' or 'distress' and so was more akin in meaning to modern words such as 'anxiety', 'anguish' and the word we have borrowed from German, 'angst'.

For the derivation of the word we have to go back to the Greek *ankhō*, 'to throttle', 'to choke', a verb which also produced the Germanic words for 'narrow', such as Anglo-Saxon, modern German and Dutch *eng*, Old High German *engi*. Presumably the association here is that if I am being strangled the air passages in my throat become narrower and this makes me feel annoyed!

The connection with 'narrowing' and the Greek verb is maintained in other cognates, chiefly in medical vocabulary. When we talk about 'angina', for instance, we are using part of the Latin phrase *angina pectoris*, which means 'narrowing of the chest'. On the other hand, when a Russian says he is suffering from *angina* he means he has what an English person would refer to as 'tonsillitis'. Both terms suggest constriction of the passageways, but to the English they are in the chest and to the Russians they are in the throat. A Russian who wants to tell us that he or she has what we

19

would call angina will use the expression *stenokardia*, which is a Greek word taken into Russian and meaning literally 'narrowing of the heart'.

ANTHOLOGY

The Ancient Greeks used the word *anthologia* when referring to collections of short poems, although the word comes from *anthos*, 'flower' (as in 'polyanthus', meaning 'many flowers'), and the verb *anthologeō*, 'to gather flowers'. The link between poems and flowers is the fact that to the Greek mind beautiful, delicate flowers could symbolize the finer feelings expressed in skilfully written poetry. The association is further underlined by our word 'posy', which is a corruption of the word 'poesy', originally the process of writing poetry.

The word 'poem' itself is from the Greek *poieō*, 'to make', and simply means 'something that has been made up', and the word 'poet' is from *poiētēs*, 'maker'.

'Verse' used as a synonym to 'poetry' is derived from the Latin *versus*, 'row', 'line', and the verb *vertere*, 'to turn', the implication here being that poetry was divided into lines of clearly defined metrical length. On the other hand, 'prose' had no such formulaic construction and was written as spoken without rhyme or metre. Such writing was described in Latin as *prosa oratio* (earlier *prorsa oratio*) which literally meant 'straight, unadorned speech'.

We can also speak of 'a verse' meaning a section of a longer poem. This can alternatively be referred to as a 'stanza', a word borrowed directly from Italian with the literal meaning of a 'stopping place' or 'room' and can be traced back etymologically to the Latin verb *stare*, 'to stand'. So, presumably, a 'stanza' was originally thought of as a section of a poem which could stand alone thematically from the whole.

ANTIQUE

Originally this word was written 'antic' in English and only acquired its present form, under French influence, in 1700.

It is derived from the Latin *antiquus* or *anticus*, which simply meant 'old', 'earlier' or 'former'. But the Latin word is a compound made up of *ante*, 'before' and the suffix *-icus*, and Wyld suggests that the suffix is derived from the Indo-European root AK, 'to see', and is thus related to words such as Latin *oculus*, Slavonic *oko* and the English 'eye'. If this theory is correct it means that the real meaning of the word 'antique' is 'with the eyes turned to the past'.

Wyld also states that the combination *ante* and *oculus* produced a Low Latin description *antocularem ramum*, literally, 'the branch in front of the eye', referring to the lowest branch of a stag's horn. This then passed into Old French as *antoillier*, into Middle English as *auntelere* and then into modern English as 'antler'. So 'antique' and 'antler' share a common origin.

APPETITE

An 'attack' of hunger, from the Latin infinitive *appetare*, 'to attack'. And 'hunger' is thought to be cognate with the Sanskrit *kuñch*, 'to contract', as we imagine the stomach does when we feel the pangs of hunger.

'To starve' is basically the same word as the German *sterben*, 'to die', so when we say that we are 'starving with hunger' we are really saying that we are 'dying of hunger'.

'Thirst', on the other hand, is really just another word for 'dryness' from the Greek *tersomai*, 'to become dry', and as such is cognate with such words as 'torrid' and 'terrace', the latter being derived from Latin *terra* meaning '(dry) land'

APPLAUSE

If we wish to show our appreciation, particularly in an area of public display such as a theatre, we applaud the person concerned. Frequently such a demonstration of approval is accompanied by hand-clapping, and this practice reveals the origin of the word.

The Latin verb *plaudo, plaudere, plausi, plausum* was used to describe the action of striking the hands together or stamping the feet when dancing. The addition of the prefix *ad-*, 'to', indicated that the clapping was directed in the direction of a particular person, and this prefix eventually changed to *ap-*, producing another verb, *applaudo, applaudere, applausi, applausum*, 'to express approval by clapping', the meaning which has given us the modern English form.

But *plaudo*, the first-person singular of the basic Latin verb, had an alternative form *plodo*. This combined with the prefix *ex-*, 'off', to produce the verb *explodo, explodere, explosi, explosum*, used as an expression of strong disapproval. In the context of the theatre it meant 'to drive off the stage with suitable accompanying noise'. This then found its way into Old French as *exploder*, 'to publicly disgrace', and this in turn produced the English verb 'to explode'.

There is an additional interesting linguistic point here. The phrasal verb 'to go off' can be used literally as in the meaning of the original Latin reference to an unpopular actor leaving the stage to roars of disapproval. But in modern English we can also talk about a bomb 'going off', presumably accompanied by a loud noise, hence the metaphorical meaning of the verb 'to explode'.

ARGUMENT

We have adopted this word into English from the Latin infinitive *arguere*, meaning 'to put into a clear light', 'to make clear'. The Latin verb in its turn was from the Greek adjective *argos*, which has a linguistically and psychologically very interesting history.

The basic meaning of the word *argos* is 'bright', 'shining', 'glistening'. But it also means 'swift-footed', the connection between the two concepts being that the Greeks associated rapid motion with flickering light. Hence 'to argue' originally meant 'to discuss in order to throw light on to a subject'.

And *argos* is cognate with *arguros*, an adjective meaning 'silver', derived from the noun *argentum*, from which the country Argentina derived its name. The main river in Argentina is the River Plate, or el Río de Plata, which in Spanish means 'the silver river'. But the story doesn't end there because the Spanish word *plata* (silver) is from the Greek word *platos* and this in turn is from *plastos*, 'can be

AUCTION

A sale of goods during which the price continually increases until the maximum price someone is prepared to pay has been reached. The increases reflect the origin of the word in the Latin *auctio*, 'an increase', from the verb *augeo, augere, auxi, auctum*, 'to grow'.

A 'Dutch auction' is one at which the process is reversed and the auctioneer offers a lot at a high price and keeps on reducing it until a buyer is found.

AUSPICIOUS

The dictionary definition of this word is 'favourable', 'of good omen', and it has its origins in the Roman habit of putting great faith in those who claimed to foretell the future by divination. The word 'auspicious' is from the Latin *auspex*, which had originally been *avispex*, a compound of *avis*, 'bird', and *specio*, 'to look at', as the word literally meant 'one who observes the flight of birds'.

Other words which have come into English from the verb *specio* include 'spectator', 'spectacle' and 'speculator', which was originally a military term meaning 'scout' or 'spy'.

The Greek verb cognate with *specio, specere, spexi* is *skeptomai*, 'I examine', 'I consider carefully', and this has given us our word 'sceptic'.

AUTHENTIC

Synonymous with 'genuine', an object described as 'authentic' is real, that is to say not a copy or fake. The word is derived from the Greek adverb *autoentei*, meaning 'with one's own hands', and its associated noun *authentēs*, which could be applied to a craftsman who had produced an artefact without the help of others. More often, however, it meant 'murderer', especially someone who had performed the deed himself rather than arrange for someone else to do it.

b

BALD

Now taken to mean lacking in or totally without covering hair, the word 'bald' originally meant 'having a white patch' or even simply 'white'. Evidence of this is seen in the 'bald eagle' which is not 'bald' at all but does have a white, fully feathered head.

The word's immediate antecedent is the Middle English *balled*, which was derived from *ball*, 'a white spot', a word which survives in Irish Gaelic with the same spelling and can mean a 'spot' in general but is frequently used to refer to the white spot on a horse's head. It is also cognate with the Russian *beliy*, 'white', the Greek *phalios*, 'having a white patch on the forehead', and Homeric Greek *phalos,* that extra piece of a hero's helmet which may have been just for additional protection but also may have held a feather or plume as a mark of distinction or identity. Further cognates are seen in languages such as Lithuanian and Latvian which have, respectively, *balti*, 'to become white', and *balts*, 'white', words which account for what English speakers refer to as the Baltic Sea.

There is an additional dimension to the etymological heritage of this word. Modern Icelandic has *bál*, which means both 'heavy frost' and 'camp fire'. The association between 'whiteness' and a heavy frost needs no explanation. But the allusion to the camp fire is interesting since there is yet another cognate, the Anglo-Saxon for 'flame', *bael*, with its linguistic resonance in the technical term for the white flash on a horse's head, a 'blaze'.

In the nineteenth century another use of this word appeared. Probably on account of the visual similarity between the white spot of a horse's head and the mark left by an axe on a tree trunk, the term for such a mark was also a 'blaze'. One of the easiest ways of indicating to others how far and in what direction a hunter or explorer had ventured into a forest was to leave such 'blazes' on the surrounding vegetation. Hence the expression 'blazing a trail'.

BANSHEE

If we say that somebody is 'screaming like a banshee' we are, probably without realizing it, using a word that entered English out of the mists of Celtic mythology. The word 'banshee' is the anglicized form of the Irish Gaelic *bean sidhe* where *bean* is the word for 'woman' and *sidhe* is the genitive case of *siodh* which means 'a fairy hill' or 'an abode of the fairies', so the term literally denotes a woman who lives in the dwelling of the fairies. This supernatural creature was reputed to wail and scream as she combed her flowing red hair, and the sight of her was a warning of impending catastrophe and death.

BARBARIAN

Used now as a synonym for an individual who displays uncivilized or uncouth behaviour, the original Greek *barbaros* simply denoted those people, foreigners, who did not speak Greek and whose language sounded to the Greeks like 'bar-bar-bar'.

During the time of Augustus Caesar, the first Roman emperor, the Romans took it upon themselves to side with the Greeks. The Latin derivative adjective *barbaricus* was applied to any foreigner who was neither Greek nor Roman, and the noun *barbaria* was applied to any foreign country outside either Greece or Rome.

Other related words here include the Sanskrit *barbaras*, meaning either 'stammering' or 'foreigner', and the Latin *balbus*, 'stammering'.

There is an interesting comparison to be made here with the origin of the words 'Slav' and 'Slavonic'. Some etymologists believe that the Slavs acquired their name from the fact that they were frequently taken as slaves by surrounding nations and that 'slav' is merely a corruption of the word 'slave' (from the Medieval Latin *sclavus*). Another theory, however, is that the word evolved in a manner not very different from route followed by the Greek *barbaros*. The Modern Russian for 'word' is *slovo*. Historically it had a wider band of meanings and would have been used in contexts where we would now use words and expressions such as 'sense', 'the gift of speech' and even a 'tale'. Anybody, therefore, who spoke a language intelligible to the natives of that part of the world was referred to as *slavyanin* (Slav) and anyone who could not make himself understood was described as being a *nemets*. This was originally a term for any foreigner, but it eventually came to designate one particular group of foreigners, so that in modern Russian it means 'a German'. Its derivative adjective, *nemoj*, means 'dumb', 'bereft of the power of speech'.

BISTRO

The origin of this term for a small restaurant sounds so implausible that it just might be correct. It has been argued that the origin of the term is the Russian word *bystro*, meaning 'quickly', and that it was brought back to France by soldiers returning from Napoleon's Moscow campaign in 1812. During their time in Russia they had learned that if you wanted to be served fast in a Russian eating establishment this was the word you had to shout at the waiter.

Curiously, modern Russian has taken the word back, with slightly altered pronunciation and stress, so that a *bistró* is now a snack bar.

BLEMISH

Now meaning a stain of virtually any description, this word entered English from a Scandinavian root via Old French and is linguistically linked to the colour blue. The Middle English word *blemisshen* was derived from the Old French *blemir*, 'to wound', but the original meaning of this verb was 'to beat black and blue'. A blemish, therefore, had originally been 'a bruise', and the association with the colour blue survives in the modern Icelandic words *blár*, 'blue', and *blami*, 'a blue tint'.

The source of the word 'bruise' is unclear, but it has been suggested that there is a possible connection between it and the Irish Gaelic root *bris-*, 'to break'.

BLESS

The Anglo-Saxon *bledsian*, 'to bless', 'to consecrate', is derived from the Germanic root *blod*, 'blood', as the verb originally meant 'to sprinkle with blood'. The suggested Indo-European root here is BHLA, 'to flower', 'to bloom', 'to flourish', and if the association is correct the words 'bless', 'bloom' and 'blossom' are all cognate.

BOG

A bog is an area of soft, marshy land traditionally associated with the peat-bogs of Ireland. 'Bog' is from the Irish Gaelic adjective *bog*, meaning 'soft', and its derivative noun *bogach*, 'a quagmire'.

The association of this word with the now common expression 'bog standard' is probably incorrect. The more accurate suggestion is likely to be that the expression comes from engineering shorthand used by nineteenth- and early twentieth-century inspectors who certified industrial products by chalking BOG on them to indicate that they reached 'British or German' standards.

BOIL

Almost all the authorities agree that the word 'boil', referring to a swelling containing pus, is derived from the Anglo-Saxon *byle* and ultimately connected with the word 'bile'. But there is also a curious linguistic coincidence that seems to have been overlooked by etymologists. The Greek verb *hepsō* is the verb 'to boil', which appears remarkably similar to the word 'septic' (h/s interchange). Considering that 'a boil' is full of 'septic' matter it is just possible that there is a linguistic link.

BOMB

The word is onomatopoeic, that is to say it is derived from the sound associated with it. The deep booming noise of a bomb's explosion must have reminded its inventors of the Latin and Greek words *bombus* and *bombos* which were applied to the deep buzzing sounds made by trumpets and certain insects. Another related noun in Greek, *bombulios*, could be used for any buzzing insect, particularly the bee, and this is the origin of our 'bumble' bees.

The French for a bomb is *une bombe*, but care needs to be taken to avoid confusion as the word has other meanings. For instance, it can be used for a spray or what we would now refer to in English as an aerosol, so *une bombe deodorante* and *une bombe insecticide* are 'deodorant spray' and 'fly spray' respectively and have absolutely nothing to do with explosive devices.

Spanish has similar traps for the unwary. *Una bomba* is 'a bomb', but it is also any kind of pump, so that *un bombero* is not a bomber but a fireman and the *cuerpo de bomberos* is the fire brigade. And *una bombilla* is not a little bomb but a light bulb!

A *bombardir* in Russian can either be a bomb-aimer in the air force or a striker in a football team.

BOTANY

The study of plants takes it name from the Greek *botanē*, 'grass', 'pasture', 'fodder', which in turn is from the verb *boskō*, 'to feed' or 'to nourish.'

Cognate with this verb is the scientific name for an elephant's trunk, the proboscis. The Greek preposition *pro*, 'before,' 'in front', has been attached to the root of the verb to produce *proboskis* which literally means 'that which feeds in front'.

BOW AND ARROW

These words are treated here together not only because of their functional interdependence but because they are etymologically almost identical.

The word 'bow' is from an Indo-European root BHUGH, 'to bend', 'to bow', 'to turn about', and its closest ancestor is the Anglo-Saxon *boga*, meaning 'bent' or 'bowed'. Interestingly, the same root has given us the word 'buxom' which was originally a term meaning 'can be bent' and therefore implied obedience.

The word 'arrow' appeared in Anglo-Saxon as *arewe* and was itself descended from the Gothic *arhwazna* from a supposed Germanic base, *arkho*. This in turn was allied to the Latin noun *arcus*, which is clearly related to words such as 'arc' and 'arch', and this brings us back to 'bow'.

For the Ancient Greeks this weapon of war or hunting implement was made up of three component parts: *to toxon*, 'the bow', *to neuron*, 'the string', and *hoi oistoi*, 'the arrows', all of which found their way into English , although sometimes the manner and route of their entry is not immediately obvious.

To toxon has given us the word 'toxin' and its adjective 'toxic' as alternatives for 'poison' and 'poisonous'. The poison (from the Latin *potere*, 'to drink', and the same word etymologically as 'potion') especially made for smearing on the arrow tips was known in Greek as *to toxon pharmakon*, 'the bow and arrow drug'. 'To be intoxicated' did not originally imply a state of inebriation but, rather, that one was suffering the effects of poison.

To neuron, the string, is our word 'nerve' and survives in its original form in medical words and expressions such as 'neuron', 'neurology', 'neurosurgery', etc.

There were at least four words in Ancient Greek for 'arrow(s)'. *Toxa*, the plural of *toxon*, could be used to mean either 'bow and arrow' or just 'arrows'. A variant of this word, *toxeuma*, also meant 'arrow'. Another word was *iós* , used as 'arrow' but derived from the verb *eimi*, the future of the verb 'to go'. Presumably the thinking here was that if you pull back the string and release it the piece of wood with a tip at one end and a flight of some sort at the other 'will go' towards the target. But there is another association here with poisons in that the same word meant 'snake's venom'.

The other word for 'arrow' was *oistos*, which was derived from *oisō*, 'I will carry', the irregularly formed future of *pherō*, 'I carry'. So 'arrows' were those things which a hunter or warrior would carry in his hands as he left home with his bow slung over his shoulder.

There is a further association with the verb 'to carry'. The word *pharmakon*, 'drug', 'remedy', 'medicine', is thought to be from *pharō*, a dialect form of *pherō*, and as such is a reference to the medicaments 'brought' or 'carried' by anyone coming to the aid of a sick or injured person.

It may seem far removed from 'bows and arrows', but the medical term for gullet, 'oesophagus' (which should be spelt after the Greek fashion *-os*), is probably a distant relative. The word is thought to be from the same stem as we have seen in the Greek for arrow *ios* – 'will carry' – plus the infinitive *phagein*, 'to eat'. So the oesophagus is that part of the human anatomy which 'will carry the food away' to another part of the body where it 'will be eaten'.

BRIDE

From the Greek verb *bruō*, 'to teem with', 'be full of', a reference to the children she is expected to produce. The same verb also gives us the word 'embryo', in Greek *embruon* (*en* = in + *bruon*, neuter of the present participle of *bruō*).

BRIDEGROOM

Literally 'the bride's man', but the second element is a misspelling as the second 'r' is a later addition. The 'groom' element should be 'goom' as it is derived from the Anglo-Saxon *guma*, a noun which is cognate with the Latin *homo, hominis*. This is in turn derived from the word *humus*, 'the ground', which has also given us the words humble, humility, etc. The derivative noun from 'humility', *humilitas*, for instance, originally meant 'nearness to the ground'.

If we follow this lead even further back we see that *humilis* is cognate with the Greek word *khamai*, 'on the ground', which, when combined with the word for a lion, *leōn*, produces 'ground lion' or our word 'chameleon'.

BROGUE

We use this word with two meanings. We can talk about a 'pair of brogues' in which case we are referring to a pair of stout outdoor shoes designed to give years of wear. But we can also talk about someone as having a soft 'Irish brogue' by which we mean that he or she speaks with a lilting Irish accent. The derivation of the first usage is clear; that of the second is subject to supposition.

The word 'brogue' is a direct borrowing from the Irish Gaelic *bróg*, which simply means almost any kind of footwear but in particular 'shoe'.

The use of the word to describe a particular way of speaking is thought to be simply a case of association. Those who wore stout footwear were thought more likely to be Irish and therefore to speak with an Irish accent.

BUDDHA

The founder of one of the world's great religions, Siddhartha Gautama (b. *c.* 563 BC) achieved a state of nirvana through meditation and thus became know as the 'Buddha' or 'Enlightened One'.

The etymological root here is BHUDH, meaning all of 'to awaken', 'to inform', 'to become aware of'. Consequently it has a habit of showing up unexpectedly in such geographically and chronologically separated languages as Homeric Greek, which has *peuthomai*, 'to enquire', and modern Russian with *budit'*, 'to wake somebody up', and *budil'nik*, 'alarm clock'. The same root even reappears in the English word 'beadle', who, in former times, was a parish officer with responsibility for keeping order in churches and consequently had to 'be alert' to the possible misdemeanours of others.

C

CALAMITY

From the Latin word *calamitas*, the original meaning of 'calamity' was 'destruction to crops', and some sources take matters further and state that such destruction was due to hailstones. Later it came to mean 'misfortunes of war' and then was applied to misfortune in general.

An earlier form of the word is thought to have been *cadamitas*, a form directly linked with the Greek *kēdō*, 'to annoy', 'to trouble', 'to distress', and the Sanskrit *kadanam*, 'destruction'.

There is an interesting etymological echo to the possible connection between a calamity and crop failure caused by hailstones. The modern English word 'plague', which we associate with virulent disease, is derived from the Latin *plaga*, 'blow', 'injury', 'disaster', which in turn is derived from the Greek *plēgē*, 'blow', and the verb *plēssō*, 'to strike'. But there is a Biblical reference which apparently illustrates the association in ancient times between hailstones, crop failure and disaster in general. In Revelations XVI: 21 we read: 'And there fell upon men a great hail out of heaven, every stone about the weight of a talent: and men blasphemed God because of the plague of the hail: for the plague thereof was exceeding great.'

CALCULATE

Now a verb defining the process of finding the solution to problems involving numbers, the origin of the word is the Latin *calculus*, meaning 'pebble', itself the diminutive of *calx*, meaning 'stone'. The reasoning here is clear: the earliest 'calculations' were performed by counting pebbles.

'Mathematics' is used in English now exclusively to describe that branch of learning associated with numerical calculations, but the original derivative Greek infinitive *mathein* simply meant 'to learn'. With the passage of time, however, the Greeks began to separate the study of numbers from other branches of learning and distinguished between the two by having a singular noun and a plural noun formed from the same verb: *to mathema* (singular), 'learning', 'knowledge', and *ta mathemata* (plural), 'mathematics'. The noun *mathematikos* for the Greeks meant 'mathematician', but for the Romans its equivalent *mathematicus* meant both 'mathematician' and 'astrologer'.

CALENDAR

Originally an account-book (Latin *calendarium*) kept by money-lenders in Ancient Rome and so called because people were called to pay the interest on their loans on the first day of the month. This day was known as the Calends or Kalends, from the Latin *calare* and Greek *kaleō*. Although the word is derived from a Greek verb the concept was purely Roman. The Greeks did not use calends, which is why the expression 'at the Greek calends' is a colourful way of saying 'never'.

CALLOW

This word is now almost exclusively used in the expression 'a callow youth' to denote an inexperienced young man. The word itself means 'bare' in the sense of beardless and is directly related to the Russian word *goliy*, 'naked'.

CANDIDATE

Originally a 'candidate' was someone who was clothed in white (that is, in a *toga candida*) as a sign that they were being considered for office. The origin of the word is the Latin *candidus*, 'shining white', from the infinitive *candere*, 'to shine'. Other words from the same verb are 'candle', 'incendiary', 'incandescent', etc. The word 'candid' also comes from this verb, the association being that to the ancients whiteness and brightness were associated with honesty.

The Latin for matt white was *albus*, and this is thought to be the origin of the alternative name for England, Albion, and is considered to be a reference to the white cliffs of Dover. The neuter form of the Latin adjective *albus* is *album*. The word was used also as a noun meaning the 'white tablet' on which the Pontifex Maximus or High Priest would record and publish the important events of the coming year. The tablet was also used to record the names of senators, jurists, etc., and eventually the custom evolved of asking one's friends to scratch their names on an *album amicorum* (literally, 'tablet of friends'), the precursor of the modern autograph album.

CANOPY

Strictly speaking this word should be spelt 'conopy' as it is derived from the Latin *conopium*, which in turn is derived from the Greek *kōnōpeion*, a term used to describe an Egyptian bed draped with mosquito curtains. *Kōnōpeion* is from *kōnōps*, 'a gnat', which itself is from *kōnos*, 'cone', and *ōps*, 'sight', 'appearance', etc., which is a reference to the gnat's cone-shaped head.

The noun *ōps* was derived from the Greek verb 'to see' which has a rather convoluted history. The standard verb has a present tense form of *horaō* with an irregularly formed future of *opsomai*. But there is also a rare form of the present tense, *optazō*, derived from the future, which is the recognizable root of many English words. Consider, for example, 'optical' (relating to the eye), 'synopsis' (brief survey, literally 'seeing everything together'), 'myopia' (short-sightedness, but literally 'with eyes closed') and 'autopsy' (having a look for oneself; seeing with one's own eyes).

CARBUNCLE

In modern English this word brings to mind the image of an unsightly abscess. In the sixteenth century, however, it was applied to any abscess or tumour which was also inflamed, and this reflects the earlier, thirteenth-century meaning of a fiery-coloured precious stone. The important point here, etymologically speaking, is the association with fire since the word is derived from the Latin *carbunculus*, which also meant a precious stone but originally was a term for small pieces of glowing charcoal or coal, the Latin for which was *carbo*.

The Indo-European root behind all this is KAR, 'to burn', which also has a later form of *har* and is seen in the Germanic terms used to denote a place where fires were lit. The Old High German *hert* or *herd* and Anglo-Saxon *heord*, for instance, evolved into the modern English word 'hearth'.

Every hearth needs a grate or basket in which the logs and/or coal can sit. This is from the Low Latin *grata*, a later form of *cratis*, which was originally a wickerwork basket. The ultimate Indo-European root is KART, 'to weave'.

With the advent of metal baskets, of course, the process of 'weaving' was much more difficult a task, but the basic concept survived even though it is not immediately apparent in cognate words in modern English. Take, for instance, the word 'crass'. Its most common use today is probably in the expression 'crass stupidity' but originally it meant 'dense' or 'thick' as applied to fences and primitive, wooden walls. The same concept and Indo-European root have also given us words such as 'curve' (think of how much bending is involved in weaving) and 'crate' which, after all, is a kind of basket. 'Grating', now usually associated with bars placed over a window to allow the air in and keep the burglars out, is merely a variation of the word 'grate'.

CARDINAL

Both as an adjective and a noun this word is derived from the Greek *kradainō,* 'to swing', and the Latin *cardo,* 'hinge', 'pivot', so the word basically describes something vitally important or, in other words, on which all else depends or hangs. Hence we have the cardinal virtues and the cardinal points of the compass.

As a noun, a cardinal is one of the highest-ranking officials in the Catholic Church, second only in rank and importance to the Pope.

CARNIVAL

Generally used now to describe a time of riotous festivity, celebration and enjoyment, it was originally a word with considerably religious significance. It entered English in the sixteenth century from Italian and specifically referred to the final celebrations to usher in the fasting season of Lent.

'Carnival' is comprised of two elements: *caro*, the Latin for 'flesh', and the verb *levare*, 'to lift' or, in this case, 'to remove'. The combined elements produced a word which literally meant 'the removal of flesh', for Lent was the time of the year when all flesh was to be removed from the menu, so to speak.

The original meaning of *caro* was not what we now understand by the word 'flesh'. Its application to the edible parts of meat was a later development as the word was derived from the Greek *keirō*, 'to cut off', and originally simply referred to any part of a dead animal that had been 'sliced off'.

There is also a direct linguistic link here with the flower we know as the 'carnation' because of its rosy or pink colour which was so reminiscent of uncooked flesh.

Similar in meaning to 'carnival' is the word 'festival'. This is derived from the Latin *festum*, 'holiday', 'banquet', which in turn was derived from the adjective *festivus*, meaning 'lively' or 'merry'. Both owe their origins to the Indo-European root BHA, 'to shine', so presumably the original sense behind the word 'festival' was an occasion when everybody had the opportunity to appear happy and 'bright'.

CAROL

Although a carol has come to mean a particular kind of religious song sung at Christmas it did not acquire this meaning until the sixteenth century. Before that almost any song could be called a carol, and earlier still, up to about the thirteenth century, it would have been sung by people dancing in a ring formation.

The word itself is derived from the Greek *choraulēs*, 'a flute-player at a dance', and it filtered down into English via Italian *carola* and Old French *carole*.

The Greek word was a compound noun formed from *choros*, 'dance' (and eventually 'chorus' in English), and *aulos*, a word which was used to designate almost any hollow tube or pipe which could be blown through and hence came to mean any wind instrument in general and a flute in particular. The derivative verb here is *aō*, 'to blow', which incidentally had a compound form *asthmainō*, 'to pant', 'to breathe with difficulty', and an associated noun *asthma*, 'difficult breathing'.

A relative of *aulos* was *aulōn*, 'ravine', 'gully', 'channel'. Presumably the basic idea here is a valley along which the wind would blow, and eventually the word was applied to the windy passageways between buildings. Subsequently it made its way into Russian where it emerged as *ulitsa*, the usual word for road or street. But it is also connected with another Russian word, *ulei*, beehive. The association here becomes clear when we remember that the Slavonic beehive bears no resemblance to what is thought of as a beehive in other parts of Europe. It is an elongated tube which, rather, resembles a section of a tree-trunk or, to put it another way, an extremely large flute.

CARPENTER

Modern English uses this word exclusively to designate skilled workers who work with wood, although the word is also mistakenly applied to people who make furniture. Strictly speaking, such people should be referred to as cabinet-makers.

Originally a *carpentarius* (the Latin word from which 'carpenter' is derived) drove a two-wheeled carriage, known as a *carpentum*, the favoured means of transport for the ladies of Ancient Rome. Later a *carpentarius* would not only drive such vehicles but would also build them, and this activity is the genesis of the present English meaning of the word.

Other words cognate with 'carpenter' are 'carriage', 'cart' and even the ubiquitous 'car'.

CATACLYSM

Generally used now as a term to describe any sudden upheaval and frequently as a synonym for misfortune, the original meaning of the word involved inundation. The Greek noun from which it is derived is *kataklusmos*, 'deluge', from the verb *katakluzō*, 'to inundate'. This was comprised of *kata*, 'down', and *kluzō*, which could either mean 'to be stormy' when applied to the seas and oceans or, in other contexts, 'to wash over', 'to dash against', 'to wash off', 'to wash away'.

Kluzō is cognate with the Latin noun *cloaca*, 'drain', 'sewer', as in the *cloaca magna*, the sewer reputedly constructed by Tarquinius Priscus which carried the waste matter away from the Forum and deposited it into the Tiber. This noun has also given us the adjective 'cloacal', meaning 'relating to drains and sewers'.

CATALOGUE

The most common usage of this word nowadays is its application to glossy books detailing the wares offered for sale by high street stores. The Greek word from which it is derived, *katalogos*, was a list of people who were eligible for military service. The verb with which it is associated is *katalegō*, meaning, among other things, 'to make a list', 'to select for military training', 'to enlist' (transitive).

CATARACT

This word can either mean a waterfall or, as a medical term, describe progressive loss of vision caused by a film growing across the lens of the eye.

The root of the word is the Greek verb *katarrēgnumi*, 'to crash down', 'gush forth', and the noun from it, *katarraktês* , 'waterfall'. Later the Romans borrowed the word as *cataracta* but added a couple of their own meanings: 'sluice gate' and 'portcullis'. The latter gave us our medical meaning, as a cataract is similar in effect to a grating descending over the eye.

CATASTROPHE

When things go badly wrong and we feel as though our world has been turned upside down, we have the feeling that a catastrophe has befallen us. We do not recall that the origin of the word is to be found among the farmers who worked the land in Ancient Greece. The word is comprised of two elements: the prefix *kata*, 'down', and the verb *trepō*, 'to turn'; together they form *katastrephō*, which meant nothing more than to dig the ground and turn the soil in preparation for sowing. The concept of overturning has given the word its modern English meaning.

CATEGORY

This is another excellent example of how a modern word can evolve from a linguistic source in such a way as to disguise almost totally any connection with it.

The word 'category' is a direct descendant of the Greek *agora*, meaning 'market' or 'marketplace'. In order to appreciate the long linguistic journey undertaken by this word to its modern English form, we have to understand the difference between our concept of a marketplace and that of the Ancient Greeks.

To us a market is simply a place where traders of various kinds sell their wares to the public. In Ancient Greece, however, it was a part of a town set aside not only for commercial purposes but also for public debate, legal proceedings, politics, elections and, generally speaking, for any kind of activity involving citizens gathered together for specific purposes. As a result of this plethora of uses, the word *agora* took on additional meanings. It came to denote not only a simple marketplace but also an Assembly of the People and, later still, the speeches delivered there by the public figures and politicians. Separate verbs even evolved from the word *agora* to distinguish between the various activities, so that in Ancient Greek we have both *agorazō* 'to conduct business on the market', and *agoreuō*, 'to speak in the Assembly', 'to address', 'to declare'.

The addition of the prefix *kata* (this prefix has many meanings, but here it means 'against') gives us *katagoreuō*, 'to speak against', 'to accuse', 'to denounce'. However, there was also a further, related verb *katēgoreuō*, which also meant 'to accuse', but this had the additional meaning of 'to signify' or 'to intimate' and, ultimately, 'to classify'. Hence the noun *katēgoria* which originally meant 'accusation' acquired the additional and less emotive meaning of 'classification', the meaning we attribute to the word today.

CENTRE

The mid-point, especially of a circle, the word is derived from the Greek *kentron*, meaning 'spike', 'goad' or 'prick', and was originally the point of a pair of compasses which, of course, is always placed at the centre of the circle.

Kentron eventually came to mean the same as the mid-point of a circle and thus did have the same meaning as its modern form. But the Greeks also referred to the centre of anything as the *omphalos* (Delphi was considered to be the *omphalos* or centre of the world), although the word had several other meanings. It was also used, for instance, to refer to almost any kind of protuberance such as the knob on a horse's yoke to which the reins were attached or the button-like features at either end of the rods around which scrolls were wrapped.

It was also the word used to denote the boss on a shield and in this context shared its meaning with its Latin cognate noun *umbo*. However, the Latin equivalent for the knob at the end of a scroll-stick was *umbilicus*, a word which also had a secondary meaning of 'navel' and is the origin of the adjective 'umbilical'.

CHAMPION

More often than not this word is now used to denote a winner. It can be applied equally to individuals, as in 'champion boxer' or to teams of, say, footballers, as in 'league champions' or 'European champions'.

However, the original meaning of the word was not necessarily so optimistic, as it simply meant 'fighter'. It is derived from the noun *campus*, the Latin for 'field' or more specifically 'battlefield', and the Late Latin term *campion* was applied to anyone prepared to take to the field to do battle. In the Middle Ages the word came to denote a fighter who was willing to take part in single combat in order to defend either his own or somebody else's honour. Hence we have the concept of the 'King's champion', a fighter (probably a knight) who was prepared to defend his king against his enemies.

Cognate with the Latin *campion* is Anglo-Saxon *cempa*, 'warrior', the modern German verb *kämpfen*, 'to fight', and the noun *das Kampf*, as in Adolf Hitler's account of his 'struggle', *Mein Kampf*.

The word *campus*, as we have already seen, was the Latin for 'field'. But there is a body of linguistic opinion that maintains that this word originally meant 'undulating countryside', cognate as it is with the Greek *kampē*, 'a river bend', and the verb *kamptō*, 'to bend', 'to turn'. A further noun from this verb was *kamara*, which was used to denote anything with a bent or curved covering. This eventually evolved into words such as the French *chambre* and English 'chamber' and even what we now refer to as a 'camera' (the original cameras were little boxes or 'rooms' as in *camera obscura*, 'dark room').

The association between the Greek *kampē* and bowed or vaulted constructions had another effect. In addition to producing an alternative word for 'room' it also came to be associated with a particular spot in a room where the fire was with its arched or vaulted covering. In other words, *kamara* not only produced 'chamber', etc., but another Greek word *kaminos*, 'oven', the Latin word *caminus*, 'forge', and eventually the French word *cheminée* and our word 'chimney'.

CHEAP

Now used as an adjective, this word was originally a noun (Anglo-Saxon *ceap*, 'price'), so when we describe something as 'cheap' we are really abbreviating the fourteenth-century expression 'at good cheape', meaning 'at a good price', which was modelled on the French *à bon marché*. In modern place-names such as Chipping, a village in Lancashire, Chipping Norton in Oxfordshire and Chipping Sodbury to the north of Bristol 'chipping' indicates that the town or village has or had a market at one time. In a less obvious form it also appears in the name of the capital of Denmark, Köpenhavn (Anglicized as Copenhagen), the literal translation of which is 'merchant harbour', and again in the German and Russian verbs 'to buy' which are, respectively, *kaufen* and *kupit'*. The Latin cognate noun *caupo* meant 'innkeeper' or 'small shopkeeper', but, significantly, the associated deponent verb *caupari* meant not only 'to trade' but also 'to swindle'.

A modern English expression which preserves the Anglo-Saxon

verb but in a scarcely recognizable form is 'to chop and change'. Originally this simply meant 'to sell and barter'.

Another very close relative is the surname Chapman. This was originally a term for an itinerant merchant but, by the eighteenth century it had fallen from common usage as a trade description and survived only as a family name. On the other hand, it is still with us in the abbreviated form of 'chap' as a colloquial alternative to 'man' or 'person'.

English words such as 'chap', 'chapman' and 'cheap', as we have seen, can be traced back to an Anglo-Saxon root. But the Anglo-Saxon *ceap* has an even longer history and is etymologically linked to the Ancient Greek *kapēlos*, which could be a term applied to almost any kind of tradesman. In particular, however, it described a 'retail' merchant who would normally conduct his business from a fixed point or establishment. His travelling counterpart or wholesaler, however, was known in Greek as an *emporos*. This word had originally meant simply 'traveller' and especially someone who travelled by ship. The root verb here was *poreuomai*, which meant 'to travel' but also, in a military context, 'to mount an expedition'. Sociologically the inference here is interesting, as we may safely conclude that in ancient times people travelled for only one of two reasons: in times of war for conquest and in times of peace for trade.

Now when an *emporos* needed to establish a site form which he could sell the goods he had brought back from his travels he would set up an *emporion*, the Latin form of which, *emporium*, was later adopted into English as a posh name for a shop.

The linguistic connections between travel and commerce are closer than we tend to think because so many of the etymological associations have become blurred with the passage of time. Our own very English word 'trade', for example, has changed beyond all recognition. It is never used now except to convey the idea of commercial transactions, but in fact the verb from which it is derived is 'to tread'. The original meaning of the noun, therefore, was 'a path', particularly one that had been formed by would-be travellers trampling the vegetation underfoot until a 'well-trodden path' had been created to allow merchants relatively free passage. In just the same manner, a track made by doughty adventurers smashing and forcing their way through dense forest could be described as a 'route', the derivation of which is *ruptus*, the past participle of the Latin infinitive *rompere*, 'to break'. A less important, narrower route was known as a 'routine'.

Words in English such as 'commerce', 'mercantile', 'merchandise' and 'market' are all derived from the Latin noun *merx*, meaning 'goods' or 'wares'. The infinitive associated with this noun was *merere*, a verb with several meanings: (i) to deserve, (ii) to obtain, and (iii) to earn. A further noun derived from this verb was *meritus*, 'a service', 'a good deed', 'a benefit', and this has given us the noun 'merit'.

Alongside the infinitive *merere* there existed in Latin another related verb, *mercari*, which meant 'to deal in', 'to traffic in', and it was this verb from which Mercury, the God of Merchants and Thieves, derived his name.

Both *merere* and *mercari* are directly related to the Greek noun *meros*, 'share', and its verb *meromai*, 'to receive as a share'.

CHURCH

If we compare 'church' with its equivalent in other European languages the first thing we notice is that only in English is the initial 'ch' pronounced as in 'cheese'. In Scotland they refer to 'the kirk' and in Germany it is known as *die Kirche*, with the 'ch' pronounced as in 'loch'. Strictly speaking, the Scots and Germans are more correct, as the word comes from the Greek word *kurios*, 'lord', the full expression for the location being *kuriakos oikos* or 'the Lord's house'.

Languages such as French and Spanish, which use the words *église* and *iglesia* respectively, do so because they borrowed another Greek word *ekklēsia* instead, which meant 'an assembly' and itself derived from the verb *ekkaleō*, 'to summon', 'to call forth'. This same verb has given us the adjective 'ecclesiastic' which we use for matters relating to the Church.

The people gathered together in church are known as 'the congregation', a word derived from the Latin infinitive *congregare*, meaning 'to flock together' (from *grex*, 'flock').

There is an interesting parallel here with Russian where the word for 'cathedral' is *sobor*. This echoes the idea of assembling people together, as the root verb of *sobor* is *sobrat'*, meaning 'to gather'.

The English word 'cathedral' is an abbreviated form of the Latin expression *cathedralis ecclesia*, a cathedral church, that is, one in which a bishop's throne was kept. The reason for this is that the word 'cathedral' is a direct borrowing from Greek and really means nothing more than 'a seat'. It is a compound noun from *kata*, 'down', and *hezomai*, 'I sit', which combined produce *kathedra*, 'something to sit down on', 'a seat'. Our word 'chair' come from the same root. And a bishop's 'throne' is merely another Greek word, *thronos*, which could either designate a simple chair or the seat of someone in authority such as a judge or teacher.

A chapel was originally a shrine in which the *cappa* or cape of St Martin was preserved. St Martin became Bishop of Tours *c.* AD 372 and died in 397. He is reputed to have given half of his cape to a beggar in Amiens and to have seen a vision of Christ.

A 'shrine' was originally a repository for a saint's relics and only took on the added meaning of a type of church after the seventeenth century. The word has come into English via Anglo-Saxon (*scrín*, 'chest', 'box') from Latin *scrinium*, which was originally a chest for keeping scrolls and other documents in.

A synagogue, now used exclusively for adherents of the Jewish faith, echoes linguistically the idea of gathering people together as a group. *Sun* is the Greek for 'with' and *agō* means 'to bring', 'to lead', the idea being that people can be 'brought' together so that they can be 'with' others.

The Muslim place of worship, the mosque, is in its Arabic form *masjid*, derived from the verb *sajada*, 'to adore', 'to prostrate oneself'.

CLERGY

The words 'clergy', 'clergyman', 'cleric' and 'clerk' are all descendants of the same Greek word *klēros*, which could mean any of 'lot' (as in casting lots), 'portion' or 'inheritance'. This noun was in turn is thought to be derived from the verb *klaō*, 'to break off'(transitive), 'to smash to pieces', and is related to another noun, *klasma*, 'fragment', 'that which has been broken off'. These *klasmata* could be any old broken bits of twig, potsherds, etc., which in Homer's time were used for the casting of lots to see who should inherit what property and/or tract of land.

The Biblical idea, however, was somewhat different. The Levites, the Hebrew tribe from whose numbers the priests were drawn, were not allowed to inherit property or land, as we see in Deuteronomy 18:2: 'Therefore shall they have no inheritance among their brethren: the Lord is their inheritance, as he hath said unto them.' So, historically, priests and clergymen were those whose lot it was not to inherit worldly goods or land but to regard the word of God as their only inheritance.

Our concept of a clerk as an office worker skilled in penmanship and the keeping of accounts dates from the seventeenth century. Prior to that the word 'clerk' was inextricably connected with the Church, as it was the 'clerics' who had a monopoly on learning. So when the need arose to find a term for an employee with what we now refer to as office skills the 'clerk' was adopted and the ecclesiastical associations were overlooked.

The word 'priest' has come down to us from the Greek adjective *presbus* which, when used as a noun, meant nothing more than 'old man'. It was really the superlative form of this adjective, *presbuteros*, 'oldest', which gave us the word 'priest' because of the additional meaning which the word acquired in Greek society. As age was respected for its accumulated experience and wisdom, *presbuteros* came to mean not merely 'oldest' but also 'respected', 'honoured', 'revered'. This 'reverence' afforded to the older generation begat another term of address, 'reverend' (from the Latin *reverendus*, 'he who inspires respect'). The word *presbuteros*, of course, is the derivation of the term 'Presbyterian Church' which, unlike the Episcopal Church, governed by bishops, is administered by a presbytery or Council of Elders.

A 'vicar' is now associated in most people's minds with the Protestant Church, although the original use of the word in ecclesiastical circles was more associated with the Roman Catholic branch of Christianity. 'Vicar' is derived from the Latin noun *vicarius*, which originally was a term for an under-slave. It eventually came to denote any deputy or stand-in and was adopted in the fourteenth century by the Church authorities who referred to the Pope as the Vicar of Christ, a reflection of how they regarded the Pope as Christ's 'deputy' on earth.

In English parish churches the vicar's assistant is the 'curate', a little word which has seen its original meaning alter considerably with the passage of time. A curate was originally a person who had been entrusted with the onerous task of caring for the souls of others and was the incumbent fulfilling the role of the modern vicar. Its Latin derivative verb is *curare*, which meant 'to care for', 'to attend', rather than 'to heal' as the word implies in its modern English form, 'to cure'.

The confusion that has arisen in English between the respective roles of the vicar and curate stands in sharp contrast to the situation in France where the original distinction has been preserved so that the French for 'vicar' is *curé* (curate) and a 'curate' in French is *vicaire*.

COLLEEN

This is an anglicized form of the Irish Gaelic *an cailín*, 'the girl'. The interesting thing about this word is that, although it denotes a female, it is itself grammatically masculine. This, however, is not all that unusual in languages that attribute gender to all nouns. The word for 'girl' in German, for instance, is *das Mädchen* (a neuter noun) and in Russian the words *dyádya*, 'uncle', *dédushka*, 'granddad', and *muzhchína*, 'man', are all declined as feminine nouns.

CONFECTIONERY

This word is now almost exclusively associated in our minds with sweets and chocolates, but this would not always have been the case. The word is a compound noun which has come to us from the Latin *cum*, 'with', and *facere*, 'to do', 'to make', which produced a further verb *conficere*, 'to put together', 'to prepare'. Originally the word could be applied to almost any manufacturing process involving a combination of basic materials and thus could describe the work performed by such diverse tradesmen as chemists and tailors. Only in the sixteenth century did the word acquire the narrower meaning which it retains today.

In Spanish the original Latin word took a different route so that the verb *confeccionar* retains the earlier English meanings but has completely dropped the association with dainty delicacies. *Confeccionar* can be used in the pharmaceutical sense of mixing drugs, but its principal meaning is 'to make clothes'. Thus a *confeccionista* is a tailor and the *industria de confección* is not a chocolate factory but what we colloquially refer to as 'the rag trade'. A sign in a Madrid shop window announcing *de confección* does not betoken a sweetshop but a clothes shop where off-the-peg suits can be bought. 'Sweets' in Spanish are *caramelos* (not just caramels) or *golosinas*, and a sweetshop is a *tienda de golosinas*.

French uses the word exclusively in a tailoring context. A *magasin de confection* sells ready-made clothes, and if a woman says that her husband *achète tout en confection* it means that he buys all his clothes off the peg.

CONSIDER

The basis of this word is the Latin noun *sidus*, meaning either an individual star or a constellation. The infinitive derived from the noun was *considerare*, 'to meditate', 'to reflect upon', and this provided the meaning which we attach to the word today. But the original meaning was nothing more than to gaze at the stars. Presumably stargazing induced reflection and contemplation.

CONSTIPATION

An Ancient Greek naval warfare formation was known as a *neōn stiphos* or 'close formation of ships', where *neōn* was the genitive plural of *naus*, 'ship', and *stiphos* was, generally speaking, a term for almost anything pressed or compacted together. The verb from which *stiphos* was derived is *steibō*, 'to walk on', 'to trample', and so the basic idea of compactness here is associated with stamping on and pressing down with the feet.

Steibō appeared in Latin as *stipare* with a similar meaning of 'to pack closely'. Both verbs are thought to be linked with the Indo-European root STI, 'to stiffen', 'to become thick', and as such are therefore cognate with words such as English 'stone' and German *Stein* (compacted earth) and can also be seen in the Greek noun *stia*, 'pebble'. A further, more distant etymological link is with the Russian *stená*, meaning 'wall', and a link between the Russian and the Greek is found in Serbo-Croat where the word *stijena* means 'stone'.

A compound of the Latin infinitive *stipare* was *constipare*, 'to press together', and this has given us our modern medical term 'constipation', which we now see is really just another word for 'compacted'.

The Spanish word *constipado* is etymologically identical, but the meaning is quite different. Somebody described in Spanish as being *constipado* is suffering from a bad cold or influenza. What an Englishman means by 'constipated' is described as *estreñido* in Spanish, a word derived from the Latin *stringo, stringere, strinxi, strictum* meaning 'to bind', 'to tie', which has also given us words such as 'strict', 'stricture' and 'stringent'.

CONTEMPLATE

The root of this word is 'temple' and the Latin infinitive associated with it *contemplari*, 'to mark out an enclosure', 'to conduct a survey', 'to consider carefully'. Again Greek raises its beautiful head here as we see that the Latin word for temple, *templum*, is derived from the Greek *temenos*, a sacred enclosure, a piece of land 'cut off' (Greek *temnō*, 'I cut') from the surrounding area.

COSMOS

The Ancient Greeks' version of the story of creation is that first there was *chaos* or disorder and that this was eventually followed by *kosmos*, order. Also, to the Greek mind the concepts of order and beauty were inseparable, so anything that was orderly and harmonious was considered beautiful. Cosmetics, therefore, are products designed to produce (or restore) order and harmony and thus simultaneously make something or someone appear beautiful. A similar association between adornment and the universe existed in Latin. *Mundus* as an adjective meant 'refined' or 'elegant' but as a noun meant 'adornment', 'universe' or 'the world'. Modern Romance languages such as French and Spanish have adopted this word to designate the earth and thus have *monde* and *mundo* respectively.

Modern English now uses the word 'cosmos' to designate the universe and within this universe are thousands if not millions of galaxies, where again Greek has provided the word to define the concept. We call our galaxy 'the Milky Way', but we are frequently oblivious to the tautological (Greek *ta auta* = the same things + *legō* = I say) nature of our words. The word 'galaxy' is derived from the Greek word *gala* meaning 'milk'. The association with milk refers back to the Greek myth according to which Zeus' wife, Hera, was duped into suckling the dragon that guarded the Apples of the Hesperides. When she realized her mistake she thrust it violently away from her breast and the drops of milk that were spilt became the stars of the night sky.

Other heavenly bodies also take their names from Ancient Greek. A 'comet', for instance, takes its name from *komētēs*, meaning 'long-haired', derived from the verb *komaō*, 'to let the hair grow long'. The noun for 'hair' was *komē*, which also gave us the biological term 'coma' for the tuft of silky hairs which can be seen growing from the ends of some seeds.

The word 'planet' is from the Greek verb *planaomai*, 'to wander', 'to roam', 'to go astray', and is the same word etymologically as 'plankton', the term for those microscopic organisms that drift on the surface of the sea.

The Latin word *satelles*, 'an attendant', has given us 'satellite', although we now have two words for the same object, as the Russian *sputnik* has been commonly used in English since the 1960s. A *sputnik* is literally a 'fellow-traveller' comprised as it is of three basic Russian roots: *s*, 'with', *put*, 'way' (connected etymologically to the French *pont*, 'bridge', and English 'path'), and -*nik*, a common noun suffix similar to -*er* in English.

Meteoros, the Greek for 'suspended in the air', from the verb *meteorizō* 'to lift high', has given us our word 'meteor'.

The most fascinating etymology here is the word 'star'. The immediate antecedents of the word are the Greek and Latin infinitives *stornumi* and *sternere*, meaning 'to spread out' (transitive). The Latin *sterno, sternere, stravi, stratum* has given us the word 'stratum' as an alternative for 'layer', that is, 'something which has been spread out'. But it has also given us the word 'street', a word derived from the Latin phrase *strata via*, meaning 'paved way'. The Indo-European root here is STAR, meaning 'to sprinkle', 'to spread', which has given us the word 'star' via the Greek *astēr*. The reasoning here is that the ancients believed that the stars were responsible for 'sprinkling' light down from the skies.

Another cognate is 'straw' with the literal meaning of 'that which has been spread or strewn'.

COSTERMONGER

The word was originally 'costerd-monger' and meant a 'seller of costerds' (or 'costards'), an old word for apples. It is also generally presumed that 'costard' is derived from the French *côte*, 'rib', as this type of apple was marked by what appeared to be ribs.

The word 'monger' has a very interesting history. It has come down to us from Latin *mango*, which meant 'a salesman' and in particular 'a slave-trader'. This in turn was derived from the Greek *manganon*, a word used to describe any device for or means of bewitching or tricking people. The related verb *manganeuō* meant 'to cheat by sleight of hand'. 'Monger' is also allied to English words such as 'to mingle', 'to mix' and 'mongrel'.

COUP

The most common use of this word in modern English is in a political context to indicate the overthrow of a government. In this sense the use of the word is an abbreviated form of the expression, borrowed from French, *coup d'état* (literally 'a state blow'). There are parallel expressions of a literary or figurative flavour occasionally heard in English such as a *coup de grace*, 'a finishing stroke', *coup de main*, 'sudden attack', etc.

The word 'coup' in its present form is French, although it was derived from the Latin *colaphus* and Greek *kolaphos*, the literal meaning of which was 'a blow with a fist' or 'a box on the ears', and the Latin and Greek words were both derived from a Greek verb which underwent some interesting changes of meaning and thus had considerable consequences for subsequent linguistic evolution of the word in other languages.

The verb *kolazō* had a literal meaning of 'to prune', 'to cut back', as in *kolazō ta dendra*, 'to cut trees back'. Figuratively, however, this verb could be applied to people to mean 'to keep in check', 'to confine', and it eventually acquired the further meaning of 'to punish'. A similar and related verb, *kolaptō*, meant 'to hew', 'to chisel' or, when applied to birds, 'to peck'. This produced yet another verb, *kolafizō*, meaning 'to give somebody a box on the ears', and hence the noun *kolaphos*. So the concepts of curtailment, corporal punishment and restriction of one's movements were all associated with a basic verb and its derivatives. For a parallel in English one only has to think of the expression 'to clip somebody's wings' and to give somebody a 'clip on the ear'. The noun *kolaphos* passed into Latin as *colaphus*, and its association with punishment eventually produced the word *culpa*. We now know this word from the expression *mea culpa*, 'the fault is mine', and from the adjective derived from it, 'culpable'.

An Anglo-French legal term dating from the seventeenth century combined the Latin word *culpa* with the Old French *prest* ('ready', *prêt* in modern French) in the formulaic phrase uttered at the opening of a trial: *Culpable: prest d'averrer notre bille*, which was an abbreviated way of saying 'we think that you are guilty and we are ready to substantiate our charge'. The two words *culpable* and *prest* eventually combined and gave us the word 'culprit'.

CRISIS

When we describe a certain stage in events as being critical, what we really mean is that a point has been reached when a judgement has to be made and a decision taken. And when we criticize somebody for what they have said or done, we are making a judgement about them. The Greek word from which we have derived the words 'critical', 'criticize', etc., is *krinō*, 'to judge'.

Also closely connected to this Greek verb is our word 'hypocrite'; the history of this word is all the more fascinating because of its complexity. The word *hupokritēs* meant 'actor' or 'pretender' to the Greeks and they arrived at this from the verb *hupokrinomai*, which is made up of three elements *hupo*, 'under' and metaphorically 'underhand', *krinō*, 'to judge', and then the ending *-omai*. This ending denotes the first person singular of what is known as the middle voice, indicating essentially that the action of the verb is performed for the benefit of the subject. Putting the three parts together we arrive at the real meaning of the word 'hypocrite': 'someone who can make a judgement about when it is best to behave in an underhand way to his own advantage'. And this meaning is clearly illustrated by the passage from Sermon on the Mount when Christ commands: 'Therefore when thou doest thine alms, do not sound a trumpet before thee, as the hypocrites do in the synagogues and in the streets, that they may have the glory of men' (Matthew VI: 2).

CROCODILE

Krokodeilos is the Greek for 'lizard', and the full name of the animal to which we are referring when we use the word is *krokodeilos ho potamios* or 'river lizard'.

The first syllable is from another Greek word, *krokē*, 'pebble', but it is not absolutely clear why this should be. Perhaps the rough skin with its protuberances appeared 'pebble-dashed' to the Ancient Greeks, or then again there might be some connection with the reptile's predilection for basking on pebbly shores. Yet another suggestion involves the Greek historian Herodotus. He wrote, probably recording a commonly held belief of the times, that crocodiles were unique in that they were the only creatures on earth without a tongue and that they ate pebbles to aid their digestion. He was mistaken about their not having a tongue, but they do swallow pebbles to form what is termed a 'gastric mill' to break food down into more manageable portions.

Naturalists will tell us that crocodiles are not the only creatures to swallow pebbles and other small objects as part of their diet. It is quite common for some species of birds, reptiles and mammals to make use of what are termed 'gastroliths' (Greek *gastēr*, 'stomach', and *lithos*, 'stone') to aid digestion. While on the subject of digestion, we might as well mention that our word 'stomach' is from the Greek *stomakhos* which originally meant 'gullet' and was itself derived from the word *stoma* meaning 'mouth'. And the Anglo-Saxon for stomach or belly was *wamb*, which has given us our word 'womb'.

CUP

The Latin word *cupa* was used for what we would refer to as a 'vat' or 'butt' for storing water or wine. The Greek word allied to the Latin was *kupē*, which could refer to almost anything which had been hollowed out and meant 'a hole' or 'hollow'. The Indo-European root here is KU, 'to hollow', 'to bulge', which also provided the Old Norse *hufr*, 'hull', as well as the word 'hive' as in 'beehive'. Yet another cognate is the word 'coop' the wooden cage in which hens are kept. The root KU also provided the Greek word *koilos*, 'hollow', which entered Latin as *caelum*, and this in turn produced French *ciel* and Spanish *cielo*, all meaning 'heaven'. The same Greek and Latin words, when they entered English, evolved into 'ceiling'.

CUPID

The Roman God of Love, Cupid, derived his name from the Latin noun *cupido*, 'desire', 'love', and the verb *cupio, cupere, cupivi, cupitum*, 'to desire'. It is not absolutely certain, but some etymologists assert that this verb is the source of the English 'to hope'. On the other hand, there seems to be no doubt that the Latin noun and verb are directly linked to the Sanskrit *kupyati*, 'to boil', 'to become agitated', and the modern Russian *kipet'*, which also means 'to boil'.

The Latin, Sanskrit and Russian words are all descended from the Indo-European root KWAP, 'to breathe out', which is also the base of the Greek *kapnos*, 'smoke', and Sanskrit *kapis*, 'incense'. These languages have obviously lost the 'w' sound of the Indo-European root and preserved the 'k'. Latin, conversely, lost the 'k' sound but preserved the 'w', which accounts for the cognate of *kapnos* being *vapor*, which entered English as 'vapour'.

CUSHION

The original 'cushion' seems to have been the Latin *culcita*, which meant 'mattress', 'bolster' or 'pillow'. This in turn is thought to be related to the Low Latin *coxinum*, which was originally a place to rest one's *coxa* or hip bone. Curiously, *coxa* is cognate with the Sanskrit *kaksa*, meaning 'armpit', and the Old High German *hahsa*, 'knee joint'.

d

DAPPER

Now meaning 'neat and tidy' and for some reason usually associated with smallness, as in the phrase 'a dapper little man', this word has gone through considerable change. Its nearest relative today is the German *tapfer*, which means 'brave', 'steadfast', and is itself descended from the Old High German *taphar*, 'valiant'. The association between bravery and neatness is open to conjecture, but it is just possible that in primitive times those who were considered brave and valiant tended to be more concerned about their appearance and how they were dressed when seen in public. This association may not be as fanciful as all that when we consider that we do, for instance, talk about 'knights in shining armour'. Few fair maidens would dream of being rescued by a knight in rusty armour! And are soldiers not required to maintain a smart appearance at all times?

Another relative of 'dapper' is the Russian *dobriy*, which originally meant 'good' but in modern Russian tends more to mean 'kind' or 'decent'.

DEARTH

This word, signifying a lack or scarcity of something, is really just an alternative form of the word 'dearness'. As far as we know 'dearth' did not exist in Anglo-Saxon but was formed during the Middle English period by analogy with forms such as 'warmth' (warm + th), length (long + th), etc. The original meaning of the word, therefore, was 'expensiveness', and it presumably acquired its present meaning from the economic association between scarcity and increased value.

DECIDE

The basic idea, etymologically speaking, behind the act of making a decision is 'cutting away' all the other possibilities. If we decide, for example, to take our holidays in the Bahamas next year, the inference is that we have 'cut away' and discarded all the other destinations we may have considered. This is reflected in the derivation of the word 'decide', which is the Latin infinitive *caedere*, 'to cut', plus the prefix *de*, 'off', 'away'.

A similar thinking process also produced cognate words such as 'precise', literally 'to cut short', implying accuracy by a careful trimming away of anything superfluous.

A modern analogy here is found in German which combines the prefix *ent-* (roughly the equivalent of the Latin *de-*) with the verb *scheiden*, 'to divide', to produce an entirely new verb, *entscheiden*, 'to decide'.

If we return to the Latin verb *caedere* we find that there is a related noun, *caementum*, which was a term applied by the slaves to the bits of stone they had hewn out of the quarries. This eventually gave us the word 'cement'.

DELICATE

The immediate ancestor of this word in English is the Latin *delicates*, which meant 'delightful' or 'charming'. It is probably – although there is some doubt about it – a Latin compound adjective comprising *de*, 'from', and *lic*, a corruption of *lac*, 'milk', which suggests that the original meaning of the word was 'just weaned from the breast' and therefore still weak.

DELIRIUM

In modern English we say that somebody has 'become delirious' when we mean that they have been overcome by a state of temporary insanity. The expression has been adopted and adapted by the medical fraternity from an essentially agricultural milieu. The two Latin words *de*, 'out of', and *lira*, 'furrow', combined to produce the infinitive *delirare*, which literally meant 'coming out of the furrow' and was a term applied to less skilful ploughmen who could not maintain a straight line when ploughing a field. In other words the inability to keep to the 'straight and narrow' acquired a figurative meaning which echoes our modern expression, although we tend to use it to refer to moral rather than psychological aberration.

The idea of following a furrow has other linguistic implications. The Latin *lira* is etymologically allied to the Gothic *laists*, 'track', 'footprint', from a supposed Germanic root *lais*, 'to follow a track'. *Laists* shows up again in the Anglo-Saxon word *last*, meaning 'a footprint', which has survived into modern English as the cobbler's last.

But this is not the end of the story. The Gothic *lais* also lies at the root of the verb 'to learn' which, after all, is the acquisition of knowledge by following certain leads and tracking down new snippets of information.

DETECTIVE

We usually use this word in modern English in a context involving the police. It conjures up images of sleuths and latter-day Sherlock Holmeses following clues to uncover the truth and discover who committed the crime.

The verb 'detect' is really just another way of saying 'take the cover off', as it is made up of *de* + *tect* from the Latin verb *tegere*, 'to cover' (*tego, tegere, texi, tectum*) which has also provided words such as 'deck' as well as the German *Dach*, French *toit* and Spanish *techo*, all meaning 'roof'. Another cognate word is the Latin *toga*, which boys in ancient Rome were entitled to wear from the age of fourteen as a sign that they had reached manhood. It has also been suggested that *toga* is the origin of 'togs', a slang word for clothes.

The verb *tegere* is from the Indo-European root STAG, meaning 'to cover', 'to put a roof on', etc., and reappears in the Sanskrit word *sthag*, 'to cover', Old Norse *thekja*, Anglo-Saxon *thecca* and modern English 'thatch'. It is also cognate with the Greek verb *stegō*, 'to cover', 'to protect', as used in the naming of the dinosaur 'stegosaurus' ('covered' or 'protected' lizard).

An echo of 'detective' is the word 'discoverer', and this also derives, obviously, from the word 'cover'. 'Cover' entered English from Old French *covrir* (modern French *couvrir*), which was a borrowing and shortening of the Latin *cooperire*, meaning 'to shut tight', 'to cover entirely' and even 'to overwhelm'.

The verb *cooperire* produced some other interesting cognates. For instance, when we talk about 'covert' operations, that is, 'undercover' military or espionage activity, we are using one such relative. Another is also a word with strong military connotations – 'curfew'. This is an Anglo-Norman word thought to date from the thirteenth century and originally referred to that time of the evening when bells were rung to remind citizens to 'cover all fires', that is, extinguish them before going to bed as a safety precaution. The original French term was *covrefeu* (modern French *couvrefeu*) where the word for fire, *feu*, is a borrowing from the Latin *focus*. We now use the word 'focus' to mean a point where beams of light converge, but to the ancient Romans it was simply a hearth. *Focus* is cognate with Greek *phos*, 'light', and they are both derived from the Indo-European root BHA, 'to shine'.

The word 'sleuth', incidentally, is from the Old Norse *sloth*, meaning 'track'.

DEVIL

In the Christian Church the devil is considered to be the supreme incarnation of evil, but the origin of the word is far less dramatic. The Greek verb *ballō* meant 'to throw' (hence 'ballistic', etc.) and when combined with the prefix *dia-*, meaning 'across' or 'at', becomes *diaballō*. This now means 'to throw something at someone' or, metaphorically, 'to slander', so *diabolos* (the noun from which 'devil' is derived) means nothing more than 'slanderer'. For comparison we should think of the literal and figurative meanings of the English expression 'to throw mud'.

'Satan' is a direct borrowing of the word *sátán*, which was just the normal word in Hebrew for 'enemy' (the root *sátán* means 'to persecute'), which coincides exactly with yet another term, 'fiend' (from Sanskrit *piyati*, 'he blames, reviles'). There is also a connection here with modern German *der Feind*, 'enemy'.

'Demon', another word used to designate malicious spirits and frequently applied to the devil, only acquired its pejorative meaning in New Testament times. To the Ancient Greeks a *daimōn* was one of the inferior gods (as opposed to the higher *theoi*), and Socrates used the term to refer to 'genius' or the inner voice that can be a source of both creativity and maliciousness. A secondary meaning of *daimōn* in Greek was 'fate' or 'fortune', a meaning which reflects the original meaning of the verb *daiō* (from which the word was derived), meaning 'to distribute', ' to allot'.

The surprising epithet for the devil is 'Lucifer'. He is supposed to be the Prince of Darkness, yet the name Lucifer is derived from the

Latin *fero*, 'I bring', and *lucem* (accusative of *lux*), 'light'. How is it possible to reconcile these two apparently contradictory concepts? The answer seems to lie in the belief that one of the early Christian writers, St Jerome, mistakenly thought that the devil was being alluded to in Isaiah 14: 12 and 13 when the reference was really to the King of Babylon. The quotation runs:

> How art thou fallen from heaven, O Lucifer, son of the morning! How art thou cut down to the ground, which did weaken the nations!
>
> For thou hast said in thine heart, I will ascend into heaven, I will exalt my throne above the stars of God: I will sit also upon the mount of the congregation in the sides of the north.

The Greek for 'bringer of light', *phosforos* (an epithet for the morning star), has given us another word, 'phosphoros'.

To return to the verb *ballō*, we have seen how its basic meaning of 'to throw' changes when the prefix *dia-* is attached to it. This illustrates a feature of Greek whereby various prefixes attached to a verbal base can produce a wide variety of meanings. For instance if the additional prefix is *pro-*, 'in front of', it produces the verb *proballō*, meaning 'to throw something in front of someone', and the noun associated with it, *problema*, gives us the word 'problem'. So a problem originally was, linguistically speaking, something that had been thrown in front of us, either literally or figuratively, which then demanded our attention.

Paraballō means 'to throw alongside' (*para* = 'at the side of'), from which we derive the word 'parable', which originally meant 'a comparison'. Over time the word was specifically applied to those stories in the Bible which were intended to convey a figurative meaning alongside the literal one. The link with storytelling did not end there as the word came to be associated with speech in general and hence produced the French and Italian verbs *parler* and *parlare*, meaning 'to speak', the Spanish noun *palabra*, meaning 'word' (and giving us the word 'palaver') and of course the place where everyone gathers to speak, 'parliament'.

DIABETES

Etymologists seem unable to agree on the origin of this word, beyond the fact that it comes from the Greek word *diabainō* and that it has something to do with the need for sufferers to pass water frequently. Some linguists think that the connection is with *diabainō* meaning 'to pass through'. Others assert that the verb has a secondary meaning of 'to stand with one's legs apart', either as a warrior preparing for battle or in order to urinate. The explanation involving legs apart seems to be the more likely if we consider that the noun *diabētēs* is the Greek for a pair of compasses.

DICE

Most people now think of this word as being a singular noun, but in fact it is the plural of 'die' and the correct singular is now rarely heard except in the phrase 'the die is cast'.

The origin of the word 'die' is the Indo-European root DA, 'to give', but it has come down to us via the Latin *do, dare, dedi, datum*, which basically meant 'to give' but also had a secondary meaning of 'to move' a piece during a board game, hence the modern understanding of the word.

The expression 'the die is cast' reflects the speaker's belief that an irrevocable step has been taken. It is a direct translation of the Latin phrase *alea iacta est*, reportedly said by Julius Caesar in 49 BC when, after much deliberation, he finally decided to cross the river which divided Cisalpine Gaul from Italy and therefore commit himself and his troops to the wrath of Rome. The name of the river provided us with that other expression we use when we make an irreversible commitment and talk of having 'crossed the Rubicon'.

DINNER

This word came into English from the Old French word *disner* which was descended from the Latin noun *ieiunium*, 'hunger', 'abstinence from food', and the prefix *dis-* the equivalent of the English prefix 'un-'. So the combination of the two means to discontinue the fast or, in other words, to 'breakfast'. The Latin influence can still be seen in the French and Spanish words *déjeuner*, 'lunch', and *desayuno*, 'breakfast'.

DIPHTHERIA

The Greek verb *dephō* means 'to soften by hand', 'to make supple' and 'to tan hide'. This produces the noun *diphtheria*, meaning leather or tanned hide; the connection with diphtheria is the soft leathery membrane which forms across the throat in those suffering from the disease.

ELECTRICITY

When electricity was invented in the nineteenth century a name had to be coined for this new source of power and, as was frequently the case with new inventions and discoveries, the scientists involved turned to Greek for inspiration.

The word they decided to adopt was *ēlektron*, the oldest known use of which is found in Homer's *Odyssey* where it is applied to an alloy consisting of a mixture of gold and silver. The alloy was termed *ēlektron* because its colour was reminiscent of that of the sun's rays which were referred to collectively as *ēlektōr*, a derivative of the word *helios*, 'sun', and allied to the Indo-European root ARK, 'to shine', 'to gleam'.

The same reasoning led to the naming of the natural substance which we know as amber, which the Greeks called *ēlektron*. It had also been known for centuries that rubbing the solidified resin produced a strange natural force which, because of the substance's resemblance in colour to the sun's rays, became known as 'electricity'.

ENORMOUS

The idea of excessive size normally associated with this word is a rather late development as it dates from as late as the sixteenth century. Prior to that it retained its original Latin meaning which was more along the lines of the modern English word 'abnormal'. The origin of the word is the Latin *norma*, 'a carpenter's rule or pattern'. This is obviously the derivation of our word 'norm' and consequently of other words and expressions denoting those things that did or did not comply with standard measurement or design. The Latin adjective *enormis*, from which 'enormous' is directly derived, had a primary meaning of 'irregular' or 'unusual' and the connotations of size were a later development.

The Latin *norma* is linguistically linked with the Greek word *gnōrimos*, meaning 'well known', so the concept behind the Roman carpenter's tool was familiarity with a certain standard on which all measurements could be based. *Gnōrimos* was from the verb *gignōskō* (the source of English 'to know') as well as the nouns *gnōmē*, 'mind', 'intelligence', and *gnōmōn*, which basically meant 'one who knows' but was also the Greek for a 'carpenter's rule or pattern'. Additionally it could mean 'a judge' or 'an interpreter', and it was this latter meaning that led to the index on a sun-dial being termed the 'gnomon' as it 'interprets' the time by casting a shadow on to the dial. It is also the origin of the mythical sprites know as 'gnomes'. These little creatures were so called because they were thought to 'know things', to guard the secrets of nature and to know where treasure was hidden beneath the earth. The modern epithet for Swiss bankers who are sometimes referred to as the 'gnomes of Zurich' arises from the not very common application of the noun to people who exert influence behind the scenes.

ENOUGH

The closest relative to this English word is the German *genug*, and both are related to the Anglo-Saxon verb *geneah*, 'it suffices'. Interestingly, however, the Indo-European root from which they are both derived is NAK, 'to reach', 'to obtain', 'to bring', and the association with carrying is further seen in another cognate, the Greek verb *enenkon*, the irregularly formed aorist tense of *pherō*, 'to carry'. In addition the Greek noun *onkos*, 'bulk,' 'burden', further illustrates the association between carrying and sufficiency which suggests that the basic idea behind the word was 'as much as one could carry'.

There is a parallel here in Russian which supports this theory. The Russian for 'enough' is *dostátochno*, and the verb 'to fetch' is *dostat'*.

EXTRAVAGANT

Cognate with the word 'vague', extravagant is from the Latin infinitive *vagare*, 'to wander', and the preposition *extra*, 'outside', used as a prefix to produce a word that literally means 'wandering outside the limits'. Somebody whose thinking can be described as 'vague' is someone who cannot concentrate and whose mind 'strays' from the point.

FACULTY

The ease with which we orientate ourselves within the environment depends largely on our 'faculties' (from the Latin *facilis*, 'easy'), and any impairment to them makes things more difficult.

We have five faculties (sight, hearing, speech, touch and smell), and deprivation of the first three is indicated by the adjectives blind, deaf and dumb. Interestingly, however, etymology shows that the ancients were somewhat indecisive in their terminology, as the various adjectives were not always as precise as they are today. The word 'blind', for instance, was originally associated more with darkness and confusion than a permanent inability to see. This can be deduced from the fact that the word is cognate with the verb 'to blend' and its association with mixing and therefore confusion. It is also related to the Old Norse *blunda*, 'to close one's eyes', and *blundr*, 'to slumber'. Another possible but not definite connection is with the verb 'to blunder' which originally described the action of stumbling over unseen objects.

If we now turn to the words 'deaf' and 'dumb' we find that the linguistic confusion persists because both these words are derived from the Greek *tuphlos*, which, believe it or not, meant 'blind'. But *tuphlos* had the additional meanings of 'dark', 'unseen' or 'dim' (*tuphlai spilades*, for instance were every sailor's nightmare, 'submerged, invisible rocks'), and with these meanings it is cognate with the Gaelic *dubh*, 'black', as in *dubh linn*, 'black pool' or, in its more recognizable form, Dublin.

FAMILY

The only point on which etymologists seem to agree when discussing this word is that there is a connection with the Latin *familus*, meaning 'servant', and a related collective noun *familia*, 'domestic slaves' or, more rarely, the 'household' in general. Skeat states that the origin of the word is to be found in an ancient language of the Campania area of Italy called Oscan in which the word *faama* meant 'house'.

FANATIC

This is someone who demonstrates an extreme dedication to a cause or belief. The roots of the word are religious and are derived from the Latin word *fanum*, meaning a temple which survives in the now archaic or poetical English form of the word, 'fane'. The word 'fanatic' is a borrowing of the French *fanatique*, which in turn is derived from the Latin *fanaticus*, which meant both 'belonging to the temple' and 'inspired by a divinity.' In its latter meaning the word softened somewhat until it meant nothing more than 'enthusiastic', and this is the origin of the present-day usage.

The religious connection with the word 'fanatic' can be clearly seen in a cognate word, 'profane', which we now use to describe irreligious behaviour or utterances. The meaning of the original

Latin word *profanus* was simply 'outside the temple', 'not belonging to the temple' (*pro*, 'in front of' or 'outside' + *fanum*).

FANTASTIC

This has to be one of the most overworked words in the English language today. Almost anything or anyone who is even marginally better than average in some way can be described as 'fantastic'. People will say that they have had a 'fantastic (= very tasty) meal', or they know a 'fantastic (= unusually skilful) footballer' or that they have been to a 'fantastic (= very enjoyable) party'. The original meaning of the word, however, was far more precise and had little to do with the meanings attached to it today.

The source Greek word was *phantasia*, which either meant 'making visible' or 'a display'. The associated verb *phantazō* was 'to make visible', 'to imagine', and a *phantasma* (a word which developed into English 'phantom') was a 'vision', a 'dream' or an 'unreal image'. The modern usage of the word seems to have evolved because of the association with the intangible and the unreal, so when we say that someone or something is 'fantastic' what we really mean is that it belongs to the realm of dreams.

FARM

Originally the word 'farm' referred to the fixed payment that was paid annually for the hire or rent of a specifically designated area of land and the 'farmer' was the man who collected the monies as they became due. The modern reference to the land and property on it dates from as late as the sixteenth century, as does the idea of the farmer being the man who cultivates the land.

The origin of the word is the Latin *firma*, 'fixed payment', from the verb *firmare*, 'to affirm', 'to settle', 'to enter into a contract'. French uses *la ferme*, obviously from the same root, but Spanish uses *la granja* which is etymologically the same as 'grange' in English. This word is now used to refer to an outlying farmhouse on an estate, but it has only had this meaning since the fourteenth century. Prior to that it was storehouse or barn for grain (from the Latin

67

granum and ultimately the Indo-European root GAR, 'to grind'), a meaning preserved in the modern French *la grange*.

The Greek for 'farmer' is *geōrgos*, a noun which has given us the Christian name George. The name is comprised of two words *gē*, 'earth', and *ergon*, 'work', and so really means 'a worker of the land'. The term 'farmer George' is thus tautological.

FATE

A word used to designate our preordained future. Its direct ancestor is the Latin *fatum*, meaning 'that which has been proclaimed', derived from *fari*, a verb used mainly in Latin poetry meaning 'to say'. This in turn is derived from *phēmi*, the normal verb in Greek for 'to say', and by a circuitous route is cognate with English 'to ban' and wedding 'banns', as they are all descended from the Indo-European root BHA, 'to speak clearly', 'to announce'.

The same root also produced another commonly (and incorrectly) used word in English, 'to fascinate'. The direct antecedent of this word is the Latin *fascinare*, meaning 'to enchant', 'to bewitch', and the way in which we now use the word retains something of the Latin usage. If we are 'fascinated' by something we mean that it grips our attention and perhaps even arouses our curiosity so that we want to find out more about it. Generally speaking, therefore, it has a positive meaning. But the Greek word from which both the Latin and English words were derived had a somewhat more sinister implication. The noun *baskanos* denoted 'a sorcerer' and was derived from the verb *baskainō*, meaning 'to attack verbally', 'to speak ill of' and frequently 'to put the evil eye on' someone.

The Romans had a convenient phrase which they used either when things went awry or when the speaker was less than enthusiastic about a certain course of action: *Fata obstant*, 'the Fates are opposed to it'. The verb *obstare*, 'to oppose', has given us 'obstacle'.

An alternative word to 'fate' in common usage is, of course, 'destiny'. This has come down to us from another Latin word, *destinatus*, meaning 'fixed' and itself a development of the verb *stare* 'to stand'. So our 'destiny' is 'that which stands before us'.

The Greeks had a typically graphic way of explaining human destiny. They took the noun *moira*, 'share', 'portion', 'lot' (connected with the verb *meiromai*, 'to obtain one's share of something') and personified it as the three Moirai or Fates and then allotted to each a particular role in deciding how a man's life would unfold. Klōthō (usually spelled Clotho, the Latin form of the name), who was responsible for spinning the thread of life, got her name from the verb *klōthō*, 'to spin', 'to twist'. Then there was Lachesis, who decided how an individual's life would be spent and what would happen during his or her lifetime. Her name was derived from the verb *lankhanō*, which meant 'to obtain' but particularly 'to obtain by drawing lots'. The last of the Moirai was Atropos, the merciless hag who decided when to cut the thread and so end a life. Her name was a personification of the adjective *atropos*, meaning 'not turning', 'unchangeable', from the verb *trepō*, 'to turn', the implication being that when she had decided to snip the life-line nothing would persuade her to change her mind.

It has been suggested that Klōthō and her association with spinning and weaving is the base from which our words 'cloth' and 'clothes' are derived.

FEE

A fee now is used exclusively in English to mean a set amount of money paid for goods or services. But the word in its Anglo-Saxon form *feoh* meant 'cattle' or 'property' and is thus closely related to the word 'fief', defining an estate under the feudal system. ('Feudal' is another cognate word.)

The Anglo-Saxon *feoh* is derived from the Latin *pecus* (Indo-European p/f interchange), 'cattle', which itself has a rather interesting history as its antecedent was the Sanskrit *pacu*, also meaning 'cattle' but actually from the verb *paç*, 'to tie up', and meaning 'that which has been tied up'. The reference here is obviously to domestic cattle 'attached' to a particular property or owner. The Indo-European root here is PAK, 'to bind', 'to tie', 'to hold fast', 'to fix', which also lies behind such words as 'pact' (a binding agreement), 'page' (originally strips of papyrus bound together) and 'peace' (Latin *pax*, a state of affairs existing when a 'pact' or agreement not to fight has been reached).

Pecus developed into another word, *pecunia*, which denoted possessions, property or wealth in a wider sense and eventually came to include money. This has provided English with such words as 'pecuniary', now an adjective used to mean 'relating to monetary matters' (but originally 'rich in terms of head of cattle owned') and 'impecunious' meaning 'poverty-stricken'.

Another related word but one which has changed its meaning almost beyond recognition is 'peculiar'. In everyday speech this word now usually means 'odd', 'strange' or even 'inexplicable'. But it has come into English from the Latin *peculium*, 'private property', and originally meant nothing more than 'one's own'.

In early English society a man entering into a joint business venture involving an initial financial outlay was known as a *felawe*. This term was derived from Anglo-Saxon *feolaga*, a noun composed of the word for 'fee' plus *laga*, 'lay', so that a *feolaga* or *felawe* was somebody who had made a contribution or investment. This is the origin of the modern English word 'fellow'.

FICTION

From the Latin noun *fictio* meaning 'forming', 'feigning' or 'assumption'. This noun is from the verb *fingo, fingere, finxi, fictum*, 'to shape', 'to form', 'to fashion'. So when we talk about a 'work of fiction' we are really describing something that has been 'shaped' in the author's mind.

A 'fact', on the other hand, is etymologically speaking something which has been 'done', derived as it is from the Latin verb *facio, facere, feci, factum*, 'to make', 'to do'.

So both 'fact' and 'fiction' stem from the basic idea of making. The distinction in modern English is derived from the fact that the original Latin infinitives *facere* and *fingere* tended to be associated with the concrete and abstract respectively. Furthermore, *fingere*, because of its association with the mind and imagination, acquired additional meanings of 'to invent', 'to fabricate', 'to devise'. A further noun derived from the same verb was *fictum*, meaning a 'falsehood' or 'a lie'. The word 'lie' in English has come down to us from the Anglo-Saxon *leógan*, 'to lie', and this is turn is a derivative of the Indo-European root LUG, 'to break', 'to bend'. Presumably the association here is not all that far removed from the modern expression 'bending the truth'.

There is a direct link here with modern Spanish which has the verb *fingir* with the slightly altered meaning of 'to pretend' and also the English words 'feign' and 'feint'.

FINGER

Gothic in origin, 'finger' is derive from *fingrs*, thought to be related to the word 'fang' and the German word *fangen*, 'to catch', 'to trap'. As 'finger', 'fang' and *fangen* are all associated with grasping and holding, the likely derivation is the Indo-European root PAK (p/f interchange), meaning 'to hold fast'. However, not all etymologists agree with this suggested derivation, and some prefer the theory that 'finger' is actually linked linguistically to the word 'five'.

The largest of the fingers is, of course, the thumb. This has come down to us from the Anglo-Saxon *thuma* via Middle English *thumbe* and is ultimately derived from the Indo-European root TU, 'to grasp large', and literally means 'the fat one'. It is thus etymologically linked directly to words such as 'tumult' (a crowd that has grown large), 'tumour' (a swelling), 'tumulus' (a grave mound). And a thimble, a device designed to protect the fingers while sewing, really means 'little thumb'.

The Greek for finger was *daktulos*, a relative of our word 'toe'. It is also directly related to the Latin *digitus*, 'finger', and this has given us our word 'digit' which can be an alternative term for 'finger' but can also be a number. Obviously, the dual meaning results from the earliest form of calculations which would have been performed using the fingers.

Some etymologists agree with Skeat that *digit* and *daktulos* are derived from the Indo-European root DAK, meaning 'to take', and that such origins reflect the role the fingers play when an object is picked up or seized.

There is another possibility. A second Indo-European root DAK means 'to show', 'to teach', and this is the derivation of the Greek verb *deiknumi*, 'to show', 'to point out' and consequently 'to teach'. Considering how frequently the finger must have been used as a pointer in primitive society the linguistic association here is at least worthy of consideration.

FIRE

The Greek word for fire was *pur* (Indo-European p/f interchange), and this spawned words in many of the western European group of languages to describe the phenomenon of combustion. French, for instance, has *feu*, German has *Feuer*, Spanish has *fuego* and Italian has *fuoco*. Some of these languages, such as Spanish and English, have preserved alongside their own form of the word the original Greek in a slightly modified form to fit in with their own spelling characteristics. Thus English has 'pyre' and Spanish had *pira* to denote fire used for the specific purpose of disposing of corpses. These languages also sometimes preserve the original Greek for more specialized terminology such as scientific or medical as in the English terms 'pyrotechnics' (the *tekhnē* or art of fire-making) and 'pyromania' (fire mania or madness). The trade name 'Pyrex' is also a direct borrowing from the Greek.

The Indo-European root of *pur* was PU, which was not only at the base of the Greek for 'fire' but was also at the base of words to do with cleanliness such as 'pure' and the verb 'to purify'. So the association in the minds of the ancients between fire and purification was not merely psychological but etymological also.

Although the impact of Greek on other European languages as far as the word 'fire' is concerned was considerable it was not total. Irish and Scots Gaelic have *teine* and Welsh has *tân*, words which appear to be linguistic cousins of the English word 'tinder'. And Latin had *ignis* for 'fire'(the origin of 'ignite' and 'ignition' in English) which is a close relation of the Sanskrit *agni*, which in turn is cognate with the modern Russian *ogón'* (although the relationship is seen more clearly in the Russian plural, *ogní*.)

If we now follow the linguistic trail from the Greek word *pur* even further, some very unexpected etymologies turn up. It had, for instance, a derived adjective *purros*, 'flame-coloured', 'dark red'. This word eventually turned up in Latin as *burra*, but now it signified the dark brown, coarse cloth of the type that tables were covered with in order to make them more suitable as writing desks. This passed into Old French as *bure* and over time evolved to mean not just the cloth but the writing desk also, and so it eventually evolved into the word *bureau*. With the passage of yet more time it came to refer not just to the desk but to the room where the work was done on the desk, hence its secondary meaning of 'office'.

But there was an even further development. The Latin word *burra*, as well as meaning a coarse cloth, also denoted almost any shaggy, hairy covering and so was applied to the coats of hairy animals. The 'hairy' association gave the name to the plant we know as 'borage' because of the stem which has a certain 'hairy' feel to it.

Modern French still preserves the Latin *burra* in its verb *bourrer*, 'to stuff', 'to pad out', and it can also be seen in the expressions *le rebours*, 'the wrong side', and *à rebours*, 'against the grain', 'backwards', and even the colloquial *prendre quelqu'un à rebours*, 'to rub somebody up the wrong way'.

Just to round things off, what about the other commonly used word, 'combustion'? This is thought to be a Latin compound *cum*, 'with', and *buro*, an older Latin form of *uro, urere, ussi, ustum*, 'to burn', taken together to mean 'to burn up'.

FISH

A word with a very long history and one which illustrates the Indo-European p/f interchange. 'Fish' has come down to us from the Latin *pisces*, a root still discernable in most of the Romance languages: French *poisson*, Spanish *pescado* (when caught and ready for sale or eating, *pez* when still alive and swimming about) and Italian *pesce*.

The fish has a special symbolic significance in Christianity, mainly because the Greek word is an acronym of the one of the basic tenets of the faith. *Ichthus*, 'fish', spells out the first letters of the Greek phrase *Iesos CHristos theou uios soter*, 'Jesus Christ son of God and Saviour'. It has also been suggested that *ichthus* is a derivative of the Greek word *thuō*, meaning 'to rush impetuously', and that the creature is so called because of its ability to dart precipitously through the water.

FLEA

All the following words share a common root: flea, flee, fly, flow; and the easiest way to explain this is by going straight back to the Indo-European root and working forwards. It should also be pointed out first of all that the evolution of these words provides a beautiful example of the p/f Indo-European interchange.

The Indo-European root PLU was basically associated with the words 'fly', 'flea', 'float', 'flow' and also 'jump'. The root can be seen in such divergent languages, geographically speaking, as Anglo-Saxon, which has *flowan* for 'to stream', and Greek *pleō*, meaning 'to sail'. It also in the modern Russian verb *plyt'*, which can mean all of 'to swim', 'to sail' and 'to float', so that the sentence *Boris plyvyot v Odeccu* could mean either 'Boris is sailing to Odessa' or 'Boris is swimming to Odessa'. Only the context would differentiate.

The association here with the insect the flea has come about because the Indo-European root has the additional meaning of 'to jump'. This can be seen in the Sanskrit verb stem *plu-*, 'to swim', 'to fly' and 'to jump', and explains the Anglo-Saxon *fleá* and the Russian *blokhá*, both meaning 'flea'. (In the case of Russian the voiced consonant 'b' has replaced the unvoiced 'p' in the combination 'pl'.)

To the primitive mind there was probably only a short gap between 'jumping' and 'flying' which probably explains why this root shows up in the latter verb as well. The p/f change has already been mentioned, and so it only remains to point out that the Latin for 'feather', *pluma*, supports the etymological evidence, and the association between this word and flying needs no further explanation.

FOLK

Modern English tends to use this word to denote simple, ordinary people whose way of life is traditional and close to the earth. We have 'folk music', 'folk dances', 'folk tales', etc., all of which suggest native influence unaffected by foreign or external cultural influences. If we say that something is 'folksy' we mean that it is informal and friendly and imply that it is more likely to be associated with rustic simplicity than genuine or assumed sophistication. But 'folk' is another word with a long history and one that has changed its meaning considerably over the centuries.

Its immediate antecedent in the Anglo-Saxon *folc*, which basically meant 'a crowd of people' but was frequently used with the meaning of 'an army'. It can be seen in the now archaic German expression *Fussvolk*, meaning 'infantry', although the same word survives in modern German with the meaning of 'rank and file'. And of course there is the modern German *das Volk*, meaning 'people' or 'nation', as used in Hitler's slogan *ein Volk, ein Reich*, 'one people, one nation'.

Russian and Lithuanian reflect the Indo-European p/f interchange here as they have *polk* and *pulkas* respectively with very similar meanings. The Lithuanian word means 'a regiment' or 'crowd', whereas in Russian the word *polk* used to mean 'a host', 'a crowd', and was even used with the meaning of a military campaign in the Middle Ages. In modern Russian, however, the word simply means 'regiment' and serves as the basis for military ranks such as *polkovnik*, a colonel, and a *podpolkovnik* (literally 'an under-colonel'), a lieutenant-colonel.

Most etymologists seem to agree that 'folk' and its associated cognates are derived from the Greek *plēthos*, 'a great number' (as in the anglicized form 'plethora'), from the verb *plēthō*, 'to become full'.

Walter Skeat further suggests that the word 'flock' is a corruption of 'folk'.

FOOLHARDY

This word entered English in the thirteenth century and was a borrowing of the Old French expression *fol hardi*, which literally meant 'an emboldened fool'. *Fol* is an older form of 'fool' and *hardi* is an adjective derived from the Old French verb *hardir*, which meant 'to make bold'.

Cognate with *hardi* is the English adjective 'hard' and both are derived from the Greek *kratos*, meaning 'power', 'strength'. The linguistic and psychological links here presumably stem from the association between derring-do and the acquisition of authority or a position of power.

The same Greek noun, *kratos*, also appears in English as the suffix '-cracy' in words of Greek origin but absorbed into English such as 'democracy' (government by the people), 'aristocracy' (government by the best) and 'plutocracy' (government by the rich).

FOREST

'Forest' in English is now a noun, but the word is actually derived from the Late Latin adjective *forestis* and the phrase *forestis silva* or 'outside woodland'. It is generally accepted that this phrase was a reference to the untamed area of wilderness that grew unchecked beyond the limits of the enclosed lands used by royalty for hunting.

The Late Latin word *forestis* has an interesting history. Its earlier Latin form was *foris*, an adverb which simply meant 'situated out of doors', although it did also have the extended meaning of 'among the people', 'abroad' and even, more specifically, 'outside Rome'. As a noun *foris*, from an even earlier form *fora*, was a borrowing of the Greek *thura*, meaning 'door', from which the English word is also derived.

If the forest was the land that lay outside the royal hunting grounds, that area closed off for the purpose was known, from the thirteenth century, as 'park' land which has survived to the present day, although the images it conjures up to modern minds is probably somewhat different. The Middle English term was actually *parrock* (a corruption of which is the later 'paddock'), which is derived from

Anglo-Saxon *sparrian*, 'to enclose', 'to fence off', 'to fasten'. Particularly, this word was used when the implication was to close by means of a beam or bolt, which explains why it is cognate with other words such as 'bar', 'spar' and 'spear'. It also has a modern relative in German *sperren*, 'to shut off', 'to fence off', as in *Sperrgebiet*, 'no-go area'.

FRIEND

This word provides us with yet another good example of the Indo-European p/f interchange. The Anglo-Saxon word *freond* meant 'friend' or 'lover', related as it was to the verb *freon*, 'to love', and its origins can be traced back to the Indo-European root PRI, 'to love'. This same root is seen in one of the modern Russian words for friend, *priyatel'*, and in the Sanskrit *prija* meaning 'wife' or, literally, 'the one who is loved'. *Pria* emerged again in its Scandinavian form in the name Friga, the Norse God Odin's wife, which produced *Frigadaeg* or modern English 'Friday'. So the last day of the working week is really 'the day of the one who is loved'.

The association between love and just friendship should not come as a surprise if we consider that modern French, Spanish and Italian *ami*, *amigo* and *amico* are all derived from the Latin infinitive *amare*, 'to love'. Irish, too, preserves the link with *caraim*, 'I love', and *cara*, 'friend'.

FRUIT

The Latin word *fructus* had two basic meanings: 'produce' or 'enjoyment'. This was allied to *frux, frugis*, which also meant fruit, and both nouns were derived from the verb *fruor, frui, fructus* and *fruitus sum*, 'to have the benefit of', 'to enjoy' or 'to make use of'.

The word is also cognate with the Anglo-Saxon *brucan*, 'to make use of', and modern German *brauchen*, which basically means 'to need' but has a secondary meaning of 'to use'.

g

GALE

This little word is a perfect example of how the etymological trail can sometimes run dry and leave etymologists disagreeing over a derivation. Skeat suggests that this word may be associated with the Icelandic *galinn*, 'furious', which in turn could be from *gala*, 'to enchant', as Norse mythology maintained that storms were caused by witches. T.E. Onions, however, simply states that the 'origin is unknown', and Wyld says that any connection with Danish *gal*, 'furious', 'appears to be merely speculative and fanciful'.

GARGOYLE

Typically, this noun is used to denote the hideous stone faces which act as water conduits around the Notre Dame cathedral in Paris. The word 'gargoyle' has come into English from the Old French *gargouille*, meaning 'throat' or 'waterspout'. This in turn was a borrowing from the Latin *gurgulio*, 'gullet', 'windpipe', and this word was derived from *gurges*, 'an eddy', 'a whirlpool'.

The anatomical associations here are significant in that other words directly linked linguistically with 'gargoyle' are 'to gurgle', 'to gargle' and the Russian word for the throat, *górlo*. And the Old French *gargouille* was almost certainly the inspiration for the gluttonous character Gargantua created by the sixteenth-century French writer Rabelais.

GAZETTE

It is almost impossible to be absolutely certain about the world's first newspaper as authorities seem to differ in their opinions. It would appear, however, that the first attempt at disseminating news by the written word was Julius Caesar's *Acta Diurna*, 'Matters of the Day', a published list of important events (including births, marriages, deaths and military appointments) which had or were about to take place and about which Caesar wanted the populace to be informed.

One of the first newspapers, as we now understand the word, was published in Venice in 1563 and entitled the *Gazeta de la novità*, which roughly translates as 'a ha'p'orth of news'. A *gazeta* was really a Venetian coin of minimal value, thought by some etymologists to be so called because of its depiction of a magpie (*gazza* in Italian) on one side.

From Venice the word seems to have spread to other countries and been adopted into other languages, albeit with different spellings and changes of meaning. The Venetian *gazeta* became *gazzetta* in Italian, *gazette* in French (and English borrowed this spelling) and *gaceta* in Spanish. The usual practice, however, was to use the word as a title (*The Evening Gazette*, etc.) rather than as a generic name for the publication. Most languages coined their own word for this means of dispensing information, some basing it on the frequency with which it appeared, others on the fact that it contained 'news' or details of events. French, for instance, coined *le journal*, based on *jour*, 'day', and Spanish had has both *el periódico* from *período*, 'period' (cf. English 'periodical'), and *diario* from the *día*, 'day' (from the Indo-European root DIW, 'to shine') and cognate with English 'diary' and 'daily'. Modern Greek uses the word *ephēmerida*, which is a compound made up of the words *epi*, 'on' or 'for', and *ēmera*, 'day', implying that the news contained therein will remain current only for a day. This word, of course, is cognate with our word 'ephemeral'. And German has *die Zeitung* from *die Zeit*, 'time', which has its cousin in the London-based newspaper *The Times*.

The Russians were something of an exception. When the first editions of the *gazeta* appeared on the streets of Venice, Kurakin, the Russian Ambassador, reported back to the Tsar, Peter the Great, with details about the new invention and the Venetian word used to describe it. This was accepted immediately into the language and has survived to this day as *gazeta*, the normal Russian word for a newspaper.

Some of the terms frequently used as newspaper titles include 'chronicle' and 'echo', words which hearken back to classical times when scholars were beginning to think about recording historical data for posterity. 'Chronicle' is an interesting reminder that we seem to automatically associate records of current events with time, as the word comes from the Greek plural noun *ta chronika*, 'annals' (cf. Latin *annum*, 'year'), which itself is from the word *chronos*, 'time'.

'Echo' is from the Greek *ēkhō*, meaning 'sound' but particularly constantly repeated, reverberating sound, as heard in the hills or an empty room. This explains why the question-and-answers approach to learning religious dogma is referred to as the 'catechism' (Greek *katēkheō*, 'to din something into one') and essentially implied teaching by eliciting answers to searching questions. It also produced two other associated words, *ēkhē*, which was either the roar of the sea or the noise made by a cheering (or jeering) crowd, and *ēkhetēs*, 'grasshopper'.

Arabic made a contribution here by lending a word which the Europeans converted into 'magazine'. This noun was derived from the Arabic *makhazin*, the plural of *makhzen*, a 'storehouse'. French preserved its original meaning in *le magasin*, 'shop', but in English it came to designate a publication in which a lot of information or articles were 'stored'.

Newspapers are now a vital part of everyday living throughout the world. Yet they can be viewed with a certain amount of scepticism, which is illustrated beautifully in two expressions, one Spanish and the other from the days of the old Soviet Union. If a Spaniard wants to cast doubt on the veracity of what somebody has said, he might say *miente más que una gaceta*, 'he lies more than a newspaper'. And the Russians used to say *v Pravde net izvestii, v Izvestii net pravdy*, 'in *Pravda* there is no news and in the *News* there is no truth'. There is a pun here in that the two main Soviet newspapers *Pravda* and *Izvestiya* literally meant 'the truth' and 'the news'.

GLASNOST
Now included in most English language dictionaries, this Russian *glasnost'* was accepted almost universally when Mikhail Gorbachev,

the last President of what was then still the Soviet Union, allowed previously taboo subjects to be discussed openly. Strictly speaking the word is Old Church Slavonic, rather than Russian, as the OCS -la- became -olo- in Russian, as can be seen in the derivative noun *golos*, 'voice'.

The same sort of change took place involving vowels and the letter 'r' so that the OCS -ra- became -oro- in Russian, as, for example, the word *grad*, meaning 'town' (as in Volgograd, Leningrad, etc.), which became *gorod* in Russian and is cognate with the Latin word *hortus*, 'garden', and the Greek *khortos*, 'a feeding place'. But the Czech word *hrad*, etymologically the same as *grad*, means 'castle'.

The Russian word *golos* has some surprising linguistic cousins. It is cognate with Latin *gallus*, 'cock', Old Norse *kalla*, 'to name', and the English 'to call'.

GLAUCOMA

A disease of the eye characterized by increased pressure in the eyeball which causes progressive loss of sight. The word is derived from the Greek colour *glaukos*, 'grey-green', and is associated with the haze which is said to cover the pupil of someone suffering from this complaint.

The adjective *glaukos* is connected with the Greek for an owl, *glaux*, a creature which figured largely in the history of Athens and the mythology of Ancient Greece. The tutelary goddess of Athens, Athena (known to the Romans as Minerva), had as one of her epithets *glaukōpis*, 'she of the grey-green eyes'. And there were so many owls in Athens at one time that the Ancient Greek expression *glauk' Athenadze*, 'owls to Athens', was the equivalent of 'coals to Newcastle'.

Glaukos had additional meanings. It meant 'bright', 'gleaming', 'shining', and is linguistically linked with the Greek verb *gelaō*, 'to laugh', and the noun *glēnē*, 'the pupil of the eye', and few would dispute the connection here between genuine laughter and bright, flashing eyes. Furthermore, the Greek roots here are directly related to the Old High German word *kleini*, which meant all of the

81

following: shining, bright, neat, small, careful. Modern German preserves the link by having *klein* for 'small' whereas English has preserved the implications of 'neatness' and 'brightness' in the word 'clean'.

Some etymologists take things even further and associate Old High German *kleini* with the Greek adjective *gloios*, 'sticky', 'clammy', 'oily', and thus claim that a further link with English is seen in the words 'clay' and 'glue'. The thinking here is that the original association was between sticky, oily objects which gleamed and shone as only 'clean' objects could.

There is a parallel in Greek which possibly lends some support to this theory. The adjective *liparos*, 'shining', 'sleek' and even 'costly', was derived from the noun *lipos*, which meant 'lard', 'tallow' or 'vegetable oil'.

GO

Unlikely as it may seem, there is a direct linguistic link between the verb 'to go' and the southern Spanish province of Andalucía. The explanation is as follows.

Andalucía was originally Vandalucía as it took its name from the Vandals, a marauding Germanic tribe that swept across Europe in the fifth century and occupied much of southern Spain before crossing into Africa. This tribe was so called because of its habit of 'wandering' here, there and everywhere, raping and pillaging and destroying all before it. And the German for 'to wander' is *wandeln*, closely linked to the Anglo-Saxon *wandrian*, which was used as the frequentative form of *wend*, 'to go'. The word *wend* now survives only in poetic language (Chaucer uses the verb frequently), but its past tense 'went' is the normal past tense of the infinitive 'to go'.

GOB

A slang expression for the mouth, this is almost certainly a borrowing from the Irish Gaelic *an gob*, meaning 'the beak' (of a bird). And when we describe a convincing, fluent talker as having the 'gift of the gab' we are using a form of the word which only came into use in the eighteenth century. Previously such a person would have been described as having the 'gift of the gob'.

Interestingly, where English expresses physical proximity by expressions such as 'cheek by jowl' and 'neck and neck' or borrows the French *tête-à-tête*, Irish Gaelic has *gob le gob*, literally 'beak with beak'.

GOSSIP

A gossip is now someone who indulges in idle chit-chat or spreads rumours and /or information about other people's personal lives. But the word has only had this meaning since the sixteenth century. Earlier, in the fourteenth century, for example, it simply meant a close acquaintance. The original meaning was a sponsor or godparent at a baptism ceremony, derived as the word is from the Anglo-Saxon *godsib*, 'related to God', and the Old Norse *guthsefi*, 'godfather'. The connection with the present meaning of the word must have been the tendency of the godparents to stand around chatting about mutual acquaintances either while waiting for the proceedings to commence or after the ceremony while enjoying a celebratory noggin of ale.

The word *sib* denotes a blood relative (hence 'sibling' for brothers and sisters) or kindred group and is cognate with the modern German *Sibben*, 'kinsmen'; both have come down to us from the Sanskrit *sabhá*, 'an assembly', 'a group'.

GRAVE

This is a trench in the ground into which the bodies of the dead are placed. The word's immediate ancestor is Anglo-Saxon *graef*, which is cognate with the German word *graben*, 'to dig'. The same word reappears in the verb 'to engrave' as both are associated with the idea of hollowing out. The basis of the words is the Indo-European root SKAR, 'to cut', and this in turn can be traced to another German verb, *schreiben*, and the Greek *graphō*, both of which mean 'to write'. If we look further back we find that *graphō* is cognate with another

Greek word *gluphō*, 'to carve' or 'hollow out' as in 'hieroglyph' (*hieros* = 'holy' + *gluphos* = 'carving'). Cognate also is the Russian word *grob*, although it does not mean 'grave' but 'coffin'.

A coffin was originally any kind of box (it is the same word as 'coffer') and is derived from the Greek for a basket, *kofeinos*.

A cenotaph is also a compound of two Greek words, *kenos* = 'empty' and *taphos* = 'tomb' (from *thaptō*, 'I bury').

A mausoleum is a particularly magnificent tomb which takes its name from the *mausoleion* at Halicarnassus in Asia Minor. This was the tomb containing the remains of Mausolus, King of Caria (died 353 BC) and erected in his memory by his queen, Artemisia.

A sarcophagus is tomb made out of stone which, the Ancient Greeks believed, would eat the flesh of the corpse contained inside. The word is from two Greek words, *sarks*, 'flesh', and the infinitive *fagein*, 'to eat'.

Another word for a tomb or grave in Greek is *thēkē* which, being from the verb *tithēmi*, 'I put', has a parallel in Russian with its noun *kladbishche* for 'cemetery', derived from the verb *klast'* (root *klad-*), 'to put'. This idea is echoed by the Greek verb *keimai*, referred to above, which was used as the perfect passive of *tithēmi* and thus literally means 'I have been placed'.

Just to complete the picture, the Anglo-Saxon and modern Welsh for a grave is *bedd*, which is cognate with English 'bed'.

GROG

A mixture of rum and water. The adjective 'groggy' is perhaps more commonly heard in English now to denote a state of unsteadiness on one's feet usually, but not necessarily, as a result of over-indulgence in alcoholic beverages.

The word entered English in the eighteenth century. A certain Admiral Vernon was in the habit of wearing cloaks (although some sources say breeches) made of a coarse type of cloth known by its French name *gros grain* which was corrupted by the monoglot English mariners into 'grog' and applied as a nickname, so that the admiral was known as Old Grog. The association with the drink arose from an order issued by Admiral Vernon in 1740 stipulating that all sailors should have their daily tot of rum diluted with water.

GROTESQUE

Now used as an adjective to describe something which is hideous or grossly absurd, the word was originally applied to primitive paintings found on the walls of caves or 'grottos'. The word 'grotto' is derived from the Italian *grotta* which itself comes from the Greek *kruptō*, meaning 'a covered or hidden place'. This has also made its way in its unaltered form into English as 'crypt', an alternative term for a church vault.

The derivative Greek verb here is *kruptō*, 'to hide', which has also given us words such 'cryptic' (as in 'cryptic' crosswords with their answers 'hidden' behind the clues) and the Apocrypha those books of the Bible whose authorship is doubtful or 'hidden'.

HALCYON

'Halcyon days' is an expression used to designate happy, calm and prosperous times when we have no worries and are at peace with the world. The expression has its origin in the ancient belief that the kingfisher (Greek *halkuōn*), or a bird very similar to it, conceived its young in a nest floating at sea, about the time of the winter solstice, and possessed magic qualities that allowed it to charm the waves and wind and thus persuade them to remain calm for a period of fourteen days. The word *halkuōn* is from *hals*, 'sea' (from which we derive our word 'salt'), and *kuein*, 'to conceive', 'be pregnant', 'be full of'. And, following the linguistic threads a little further, we should also mention that the verb *kuō* has given us our word 'cyst', that is, a pouch full of morbid matter.

Another connection with the Greek for 'to be pregnant' is the noun *kuathos*, a bulbous cup used for scooping wine out of the larger bowl or *kratēr* (which became the English 'crater'). The noun *kuathos* then reappeared in Italian as *cazzuola*, which eventually made its way into English as 'casserole'.

HALO

The halo as a symbol of power and divinity only found its way into Christian art in the fourth century AD. It had previously been used in ancient Persia as a symbol of the power and radiance of the sun, so there would have been an element of reflected glory for anyone portrayed standing next to such an image.

The word itself is from the Greek *halōs* which originally described the path trodden out by oxen as they moved in circles on the threshing floor. The verb from which this noun comes is *eluō*, 'to roll', which is allied to both 'voluble', the original meaning of which was 'easily rolled', and 'volume', which was a parchment that could be rolled up.

As the Greek *eluō* is connected with the Indo-European root WAL, 'to roll', other linguistic cousins from the same root include 'wallet' and 'to wallow'.

HAND

From the Gothic verb *hinthan*, 'to seize', and its associated noun *handus*, a hand is literally 'something that grasps'.

The Indo-European root PAD, 'to go', is directly related to the Sanskrit word *padah*, meaning 'foot'. The p/f interchange is evident again here as most languages of Europe have words beginning with a 'p' or an 'f' to describe that part of the body which is normally in contact with the ground. Latin had *pes, pedis* which are the base for words such as 'pedestrian', 'pedal' and 'pedestal'. Greek had *pous, podos*, which gave us the words 'podium' and 'podagra', literally a 'seizure of the foot', a medical term for what is commonly known as 'gout'. Modern French and Spanish have *pied* and *pie* respectively, whereas the Northern European languages prefer the 'f' equivalent, for example, German, which has *Fuss*, Dutch, which has *voet*, and Danish, which has *fod*.

HANDCUFFS

This word is a corruption of the Anglo-Saxon *handcops*, which was a compound of 'hand' plus the word *cops*, meaning a 'fetter'.

Spanish has a very politically incorrect word for these implements of restraint. They are known in Spain as *esposas*, which literally is the plural of the word *esposa*, meaning 'wife'. In other words, to the Spanish way of thinking the *raison d'être* of both 'wives' and 'handcuffs' is the perceived restriction of freedom.

HARANGUE

An Old French word which has come straight into English in its unaltered form, the original meaning of which was 'a speech made to people standing in a ring'. The root is Anglo-Saxon *hring*, 'ring', which is thought to be allied to the Russian *rynok*, 'market', and to the Cheshire town of Altrincham, the original meaning of which, it has been suggested, may have been 'old market town'.

HARBOUR

Since the sixteenth century this word has denoted a place of safety where ships could find shelter and relative safety away from the storms at sea. Earlier it was a general term for shelter, refuge and even lodgings, but its original meaning was 'a place of refuge for an army'.

The word is of Scandinavian origin. Its Middle English form was *herberwe*, an adaptation of the Icelandic *herrbarg*, the first syllable, *herr*, being the Icelandic for 'army' (cf. modern German *das Heer*, 'army') and the second, *barg*, being derived from the verb *bjarga*, 'to shelter', 'to save'. The modern Icelandic form *herbergi* still retains the original meaning of 'room' or 'lodgings', and relatives of the verb *bjarga* turn up again in the second syllables of the French and Spanish words for 'hostel', *auberge* and *albergue* respectively.

Another word from the same root is 'harbinger'. We now use this word to mean a messenger, as in the description of the cuckoo as 'the harbinger of spring'. But originally a harbinger was a man sent ahead of an army to arrange a meal and lodgings for the troops.

The Indo-European root which produced *bjarga* was BHEARG, 'to protect', and this also evolved into the Anglo-Saxon verb *beorgan*, also meaning 'to protect'. A derivative noun here was *burh* or *borgh*, 'a protected or fortified place', which is still recognizable in modern English both as 'borough' and 'burrow', a shelter for rabbits. A further cognate is 'burglar', a compound noun from *burh* and *leres*, the Old French descendent of the Latin *latro*, 'robber'.

The German for 'army', *das Heer* (from the Indo-European root KAR, 'to destroy'), is directly related to the English verb 'to harry', meaning 'to ravage', 'to lay waste' and generally behave as an army tends to behave.

Incidentally, the Dutch and the Danish words for 'harbour' are *haven* and *havn*, both of which literally mean 'that which holds' and are exactly the same word as 'haven' in English.

HARPOON

The Greek verb *harpazō* meant 'to grasp', 'to seize', and from it were derived various nouns such as *harpaks*, 'robber', *harpē*, 'bird of prey', and *harpagē*, 'hook', but also 'robbery', 'seizure' or 'rape'. These words all made their way into Latin in one form or another, with *harpagē* becoming *harpaga*, which in turn eventually showed up in Old French as *harpon*, meaning a 'cramp-iron'. Its present meaning of a spear-like implement used for impaling fish, and in particular whales, is thought to date from the seventeenth century.

But *harpagē* also meant 'a rake', and with this meaning the word was adopted into Latin where it became *harpago*. Now this happens to be cognate with Old French *la herce* and Middle English *herse*, which was the term for a triangular, spiked agricultural implement used for churning up the earth as it was dragged along behind some lumbering cart-horse. In fact it was what we now call 'a harrow'.

At some point somebody had the ingenious idea of turning one of these things upside down and using the prongs as supports for the candles during church services and, in particular, at funerals.

Eventually the custom evolved of placing the corpse on this upturned harrow and, in this context, the original meaning of *herse*, 'a harrow', changed and acquired the sole meaning of a carriage for a dead body. In other words, it became the modern English word 'hearse'. By contrast, in modern French *la herse* still means 'a harrow' and the French term for what we call a hearse is either *corbillard* or *fourgon mortuaire*.

Another commonly used cognate verb in English is 'to rehearse', and here we can see the original meaning of the word. If we rehearse a play, for instance, we go over it time and time again, just as the serfs were forced to go over the ground repeatedly with a harrow until it was fit for sowing.

But to return to 'harpoon'. This word provides an excellent example of the Indo-European h/s interchange, as can be seen from its cognate equivalents in other European languages. English 'sharp' and German *scharf* are direct descendants, as is the Russian word for a 'sickle', *serp* (the 'hammer and sickle' on the old Soviet flag was known in Russian as the *serp i molot*, the Russians calling it the 'sickle and hammer'). 'Sickle' and 'scythe' are both derived via the Latin *secare*, 'to cut', from the Indo-European root SAK, also 'to cut'.

There are some fascinating snippets of linguistic information connected with the Russian word *serp*. For instance, what English speakers refer to as a 'crescent moon' the Russians call a *serp luný*, that is, 'sickle of the moon', no doubt because of its shape. There are also some cognate words which appear in other Slavonic languages such as Croatian, which has *srpanj* for July, and Polish which has *sierpien* for August. No doubt the link here is between the sickle and the different months in which the harvest was gathered traditionally in Croatia and Poland.

It is also the origin of the *harpuiai* or Harpies, the dreadful monsters in Greek mythology, half bird and half woman in form, who were sent by Hades to snatch those souls who refused to die and carry them down to his kingdom.

HEART

The Sanskrit word *hrid*, meaning 'that which quivers', reappeared in Greek as the verb *kradaō*, 'to throb', and this produced the noun *kardia*, literally meaning 'throbber', from which most European languages derived their word to describe the pump that drives the blood around the body. In English *kardia* became 'heart' (although the Greek original survives in the adjective 'cardiac'); in Russian it became *serdtse*; in Latin *cor, cordis* (hence 'cordial' in English, which really is the same as 'hearty'); *Hertz* in German; *cuore* in Italian; and Spanish has *corazón*.

HELL

The concept of Hell as a place of eternal damnation where the sinful dead were doomed to spend eternity has nothing to do with the linguistic history of the word. The association with unspeakable everlasting torment is largely the result of somewhat overzealous Christians who latched on to two passages in the Bible where such a fate is referred to. In Matthew 25: 41 we read about the Last Judgement and are informed:

> Then shall he say also unto them on the left hand, Depart from me, ye cursed, into everlasting fire, prepared for the devil and his angels.

And later, in Revelations 19: 20, we read:

> And the beast was taken, and with him the false prophet that wrought miracles before him, with which he deceived them that had received the mark of the beast and them that had worshipped his image. These both were cast alive into a lake of fire burning with brimstone.

The etymological background is far less dramatic. The Anglo-Saxon word *hel*, from which 'Hell' is descended, really means nothing more than 'that which hides' (from the verb *helan*, 'to hide'), the implication being that Hell is merely a place that is hidden from those still enjoying an earthly existence. The Indo-European root here is KAL (with its variant HAL), which simply means 'to cover', 'to hide', and has provided other cognates such as 'helmet', 'hall' (originally any kind of shelter), 'cell', 'cellar' and 'to conceal', all of which have come down to us from the Latin verb *celare*, 'to hide'. Also from the root KAL is the Greek verb *kaluptō*, 'to cover', as in the eucalyptus (literally 'well-covered') tree.

The Russian word for Hell is *ad*, a direct borrowing from and adaptation of the Greek Hades. Most dictionaries now describe Hades as being a place, but, strictly speaking, this is incorrect as the term applied to one of the earth gods (the son of Cronus and Rhea) who held dominion over the Underworld. According to legend he was given a special helmet or bonnet, made out of dog skin (the Greek name for this was *kuneē,* from *kuōn*, 'dog'), which rendered him invisible. Hence the name Hades which, some linguists argue, is Greek for 'unseen' or 'invisible'.

Hades, the god of the Underworld, was also known as Ploutōn (Latin Pluto), 'the rich one', from *ploutos*, 'rich'. The reason for this was that the Underworld was not only a dark and frightening place but also, the Greeks believed, the place from which the rich harvests grew in spring and summer.

Other European languages are rather more prosaic in their descriptions of the nether regions. French, Spanish and Italian have *enfers, infierno* and *inferno* respectively. These words are all taken from the Latin *infernos*, which simply means 'that which is lower', 'that which is below'. In other words French, Spanish and Italian simply speak of an 'inferior' world, echoing the English term 'underworld'.

HIPPOPOTAMUS

First of all let us clear up the spelling. The '-us' ending is a Latinized form of the Greek word *hippopotamos*, and if we look it up in a standard etymological dictionary it will tell us that it means 'river horse' and comes from the Greek words *hippos*, 'horse', and *potamos*, 'river'. But there is more to it than that.

The word *hippos* does indeed mean 'horse' and can be traced via the Ionian dialect form *ikkos* to the early Latin *equos*, which developed into *equus*, the form which has given us words such as 'equine' and 'equestrian'. The Indo-European root here is AK, 'to be quick', and this produced the Sanskrit *açva*, 'runner', from which the Greek and Latin words are derived. *Ikkos* is also allied linguistically to *okus*, 'swift'.

An alternative word for a horse in Latin was *caballus* (from an earlier Greek *kaballēs*) which, strictly speaking, differed from *equus* in that it described a slow, lumbering jade or nag and was applied universally by Roman soldiers when referring to their packhorses or mounts. French, Spanish and Italian have all preserved this word in the respective forms *cheval, caballo* and *cavallo*, and the same word has produced 'cavalier', 'cavalry', 'cavalcade', etc., in modern English.

The English word 'horse' is cognate with the Anglo-Saxon *hors* and the Icelandic *hross* and can be seen in the German word for steed, *das Ross*. The Anglo-Saxon, Icelandic and English terms are all connected with the Latin verb *currere*, 'to run' (think of a 'courser'), and thus reflect the same association with speed as the Sanskrit and Greek. Moreover, the Greek infinitive 'to run', *dramein*, formed the basis of the Latin noun *dromedarius* which passed into English as 'dromedary'.

A more common word in German for horse than *das Ross* is *das Pferd*, which seems to bear little resemblance to any equivalent word in other European languages. But it is connected with the 'palfrey', meaning a saddle-horse and frequently encountered in Chaucerian English. These two words are cognate in that they are descended from the Low Latin *paraveredus*, a term used to describe a post or courier horse. This in turn was derived from the Greek prefix *para-*, 'alongside', 'extra', and the Latin *veredus*, 'swift horse', 'hunter'. *Veredus* itself is thought to be a contraction of the verb *vehere*, 'to pull' (hence our word 'vehicle'), and *rheda* (alternatively spelt *raeda*), a term used to designate a four-wheeled carriage. There is little doubt that this word is of Celtic origin and connected with the Welsh verb *rhedeg*, 'to run'.

An interesting postscript to this section on horses is provided by the derivation of two words in common use which have changed in meaning almost beyond recognition. A 'marshal', now a high officer of state and until recently a term used to designate the highest rank in the British Army, was originally a very humble servant whose job it was to look after the horses. The word is derived from Old High German *marah*, 'horse' (modern English 'mare'), and *scalh*, 'servant', and this original menial flavour of the word can still be detected in the French for a blacksmith, *maréchal-ferrant*. In a similar vein, the word 'constable', used since the fourteenth century for a officer of the peace, was originally a *comes stabuli*, a Latin term meaning 'stable attendant'.

The second element of *hippopotamos*, *potamos*, is the Greek for 'river' and is an excellent example of just how far and wide a single linguistic root can spread. Furthermore, its etymological evolution provides some fascinating insights into how the psychological and sociological development of primitive society goes hand in hand with linguistic change. Consider, for example, the basic difference between river water and sea water. Only the former was drinkable, so the Greek *potamos* spawned words such as the Latin *potabilis* and the French *potable* (which we have now adopted into English). The Indo-European root here is PA, 'to feed', 'to nourish', 'to protect', clearly evident in the Sanskrit *pa*, 'to drink', and, although not so obviously, lies at the root of the Greek verb *pinō*, also 'to drink'. It appears again in such words as *symposium*, the Latin version of the Greek *symposion*, which originally meant nothing more than 'drinking together' or a 'drinking party' and is also connected with the Russian verb 'to drink', *pit'*. Some authorities also see a link here with the Russian *potok*, 'a stream', and even *pot*, 'sweat'. And there is little doubt that the same root also gave rise to our word 'pot' (a drinking vessel) and the Irish *poitín* (anglicized as 'poteen'), literally a 'little pot' but now used to describe the illegally distilled liquor contained in it.

If we consider specifically the concept of nurturing in connection with the word *potamos* we see that its Indo-European root appears in a broad spectrum of meanings. 'Pasture' land feeds the sheep and cattle on which primitive peoples depended for their existence, and

93

the shepherd or *pastor*, as he was called in Latin, was so called because he 'nurtured' the beasts. The word 'repast' reveals the same origin, as do the words for 'bread' in the Romance languages (those languages descended from Latin): French *pain*, Spanish *pan*, Italian *pane*, etc. They are all nouns derived from the original Latin noun *panis*, which itself is from the verb *pasco, pascere, pavi, pastum*, 'to bake'. Again we are reminded that in Indo-European languages the letters 'p' and 'f' are often interchangeable, as we see that the root PA has also produced the English noun 'food' and its verb 'to feed'.

When we turn to the idea of protection associated with this root the distinction between it and the concept of power becomes somewhat hazy. It is not difficult to imagine how the person in primitive society who controlled the river and therefore the drinking water could easily exert authority and eventually absolute power over those who needed access to the river for survival. Hence the root PA and the Greek *potamos* are reflected in such words and their related concepts as the Latin *potens*, 'powerful', *potentatus*, 'political power', and the word 'power' itself . And the Sanskrit *pati*, 'lord', 'possessor', 'husband', can be seen in the Greek *posis*, 'spouse', and even the Latin verb *possum*, 'I am able', is a contracted form of the original *poti sum*, 'I am master'. If we consider the family as a micro-society in itself we see that words used to designate the figure of authority in most European languages also derive from this root: Greek *pater*, Latin *pater*, French *père*, Spanish *padre*, English 'father' ('p' and 'f' change again), etc.

Looking a little further afield, the root PA is seen in the second syllable of the Russian word *gospodin*, 'master'. As the master of a household, the *gospodin* would have been responsible for the treatment or entertainment of strangers who came as either bidden or unbidden guests, and this function is reflected in further analysis of the word. We have already seen the derivation of the second syllable, and if we examine the first we find etymological links which are no less fascinating.

The Russian word *gost'*, 'guest', is also cognate with 'host' in English. It may seem rather odd that these two words, almost opposite in meaning, should stem from the same root, but the plain fact is that they do and their history is a long and tortuous one. And, as is so frequently the case, we have to make a start by looking at Ancient Greek.

A *ksenos* (frequently transliterated as *xenos* and seen in 'xenophobia', 'fear of foreigners') had a specific meaning in Ancient Greece. In its plural form, *ksenoi*, the word was used to define natives of states which had entered into what were known as 'treaties of hospitality'. Originally, both the person offering (the host) and the person accepting hospitality (the guest) were known as *ksenoi*, but by Homer's time a functional distinction had appeared so that when he used the word he invariably meant 'guest'. Over time, as the custom of offering hospitality to strangers widened to include any hapless wanderer, the word evolved until it meant nothing more than 'stranger'. Eventually it simply became a synonym for *barbaros* or 'foreigner'.

So the Greek word originally conveyed the meaning of both 'host' and 'guest' and then added 'stranger' to the list. Its Latin cognate *hostis*, however, retained these meanings but added a third: enemy. This explains why we have in modern English the noun 'host' but the adjective derived from it is 'hostile'. By the time Medieval Latin had evolved the word *hostis* had taken on yet another meaning, 'an invading army', combining both concepts of foreignness and unfriendly intentions. This is the origin of 'host' as a designator of large crowds and explains Biblical terms such as the 'Lord of Hosts'.

Another related word in Latin, *hospes*, also meant 'stranger' or 'guest' but without any of the overtones of hostility. The adjective derived from the word was *hospitalis*, 'relating to a guest or host', as in the phrase *hospitalis cubiculum*, 'guest's bedchamber'. By Late Latin times this expression had evolved into *hospitale*, 'guest house', which eventually gave us our words 'hotel', 'hostel' and even 'hospital'.

The word used in modern English to describe the supreme autocratic figure is 'despot', and this has come down to us from the Greek *despotēs*, which had had the earlier form of *demspotēs*, itself a word with Indo-European PA as its root. The syllable *-potes*, 'master', is derived from Sanskrit *pati*, 'lord', and the *dems* is an earlier form of what developed into *domos*, 'house' (from the verb *demō*, 'to build', and cognate with the German *Zimmer*, 'room', and the English 'timber'). So the original meaning of 'despot' was nothing more than 'head of the household'.

And a 'tyrant?' The original Greek *turannos* was applied to rulers who had acquired their position other than by the normal rules of hereditary succession, and this usually meant by force.

HORMONE

This is an organic compound secreted into the bloodstream to activate specific physiological activity. The word comes from the Greek noun *hormē,* the basic meaning of which was the initial attack in a battle or war. Other meanings of the word include the first stirrings, an onset and passionate desire. For the Stoic philosophers the plural form of the noun, *hormai*, meant 'blind, animal instincts'. The derivative verb here is *hormaō*, meaning 'to stir up', 'to rouse', 'to excite'.

Another Greek verb related by root to *hormaō* was *ornumi*, also 'to rouse', 'to stir'. This had its cognate Latin verb *oriri*, 'to rise up', which had its associated noun *oriens*, the East or the Orient, that is, literally the place where the sun rose every morning. The same Latin source is also the derivation of our expression 'to orientate oneself' which meant 'to turn towards the east' before it acquired its modern meaning of to find one's bearings.

Another cognate verb was *orkheomai*, which also retained suggestions of arousal but more specifically meant 'to leap' and 'to dance', and a further derivative was *orkhēstra*, a semi-circular space in a Greek theatre where the chorus danced. This is the origin of what we now refer to as an 'orchestra'. Furthermore, the Greeks used the word *orkhētra* metaphorically to refer to territories where battles were fought, as in the *orkhēstra polemou*, which is the direct equivalent of our expression the 'theatre of war'.

The Indo-European root at work here is AR, 'to raise', 'to go', 'to move', which is seen in the name of a creature principally associated with soaring, a bird or *ornis,* in Greek, which has provided us with the scientific name for those people colloquially known as twitchers, 'ornithologists'.

The figurative interpretation of the expression 'to rise up' can be seen in another cognate noun, 'origin'.

HUBRIS

Most dictionaries simply state that this is a term borrowed from Greek and denotes excessive, arrogant pride. This is perfectly correct, but it is far from being the whole picture.

To the Ancient Greeks *hubris* was a destructive quality which equated in large measure to the later Christian concept of sin and had connotations of violence, aggression and riotousness; it was a word used to convey such concepts as we would intend by the use of the expression 'assault and battery'. Indeed, the Athenian legal system interpreted *hubris* as aggravated personal assault which could easily lead to a citizen being prosecuted in a court of law.

Students of Greek drama will recognize *hubris* as the downfall of many a character who would then be faced with his *nemesis,* the displeasure and revenge of the gods, personified as the Goddess of Retribution. *Nemesis* is derived from the verb *nemesizomai,* 'to be displeased with'.

When *hubris* made its way into Latin a curious change of meaning occurred. It produced the word *hibrida,* which had three meanings: (i) offspring of a tame sow and a wild boar, (ii) one born of a Roman father and foreign mother, and (iii) one born of a freeman and a slave. The common denominator here was sexual union between different groups, possibly involving violence and rape. This may be largely supposition, but it still gave us another modern English word, 'hybrid'.

HUSSAR

Etymologists differ on the origin of this word. Some believe that it is the same word virtually as 'corsair', 'plunderer', which borrowed into Old Serbian from the Italian *corsaro* and then eventually found its way into Hungarian as *huszar.*

Others maintain that it is derived from the Hungarian for twenty, *húsz*, and the fact that in the fifteenth century the then king of Hungary and Bohemia raised a corps of light cavalry by issuing a proclamation that one in every twenty men in villages throughout the land had to join the ranks of this new corps.

HYGIENE

Hardly anyone would think of using this word now as anything other than an alternative to 'cleanliness', but the original meaning of the word was 'health', derived as it is from the Greek word for health, *hugieia*. Its Latin cognate *sanus* (Indo-European h/s interchange) underwent a similar shift of meaning in that it has given us words such as 'sanitation', 'unsanitary', etc., which conjure up concepts of cleanliness rather than health, although we now know that there is a causal relationship between the two. *Sanus*, of course, is also the word from which we have derived the notion of sanity, but this, too, has undergone a certain evolution of meaning. To the Romans *sanus* meant 'fit', 'healthy', 'sound of body', as did the English derivative 'sane' until relatively recently. Only in the seventeenth century did it come to be applied to mental stability alone.

The Greek *hugieia* is derived from the Indo-European root WAG, 'to be strong', 'vigorous', 'wide awake', and is cognate with the Sanskrit *ugras*, 'vigorous'. The same root also produced the Latin infinitives *vegere* and *vegetare*, which are associated with growth and animation and have given us the words 'vegetable', 'vegetation', etc.

A variation of the Indo-European root WAG was WAKS, which was also associated with growth and has given us a further derivative in the now archaic verb 'to wax' (grow) which survives in poetry and one or two expressions such as 'the waxing moon', 'to wax eloquent', etc.

HYPOCHONDRIAC

This is one of those words which enjoy tortuous histories but which offer endless fascination to anyone interested in language. We now apply the term 'hypochondriac' to anyone who imagines that he or she has every medical complaint in the book. But the surprising thing is that it comes from a Greek word meaning 'porridge' or 'gruel'.

The Greek word *khondros* had several meanings. It meant 'corn', 'grain', 'groats', but also the sticky, gluey drink made out of these groats which was similar in appearance and texture to our porridge.

Now the Greeks thought that this gooey mess resembled the cartilaginous mass found in humans behind the breastbone and between the false ribs and the navel. The resemblance was so great, in fact, that they actually used the word *khondros* to mean 'cartilage' and termed this soft part of the anatomy the *hupokhondrion* (or, more frequently, using the plural form, *ta hupokhondria*) which literally means 'that which is below the cartilage'.

The connection between the Greek concepts concerning the geography of the human body and the modern English word is easily explained. Until fairly recently it was believed that this soft area behind the breastbone was the seat of all illness.

i

IDEA

This little word has to qualify as one of the most interesting for illustrating how far linguistic tentacles can spread. The word itself is derived from the Greek infinitive *idein*, 'to see' (which had a much older form *widein*), and is directly connected to Latin *videre*, the verb which has provided us with everyday words such as 'vision', 'video', 'visual', 'television', etc. But the story does not end there. The perfect tense of the Greek verb was *oida* ('I have seen') and this was used as the present tense of the verb 'to know'. The basic concept here was that to have seen something and be familiar with it constitutes knowing it.

This *oida/video* connection also shows up in other languages such as Sanskrit which has the *Vedas* (the Hindu Book of Knowledge) and the Old English word 'wit', to know, which in turn is at the root of the word 'witch'. So a witch is really nothing more than a woman who 'knows things'.

INK

Together with the French word *encre* and Latin *causticum*, 'ink' can be traced back to the Greek *enkaustikos*, 'burnt in', and the verb *kaiō*, 'to burn'. The reason for this association is that the primitive substance used for writing was believed to 'burn' an impression into the parchment.

By a tortuous route this word is also a distant relative of the English 'calm'. The Low Latin *cauma* referred to the heat of the sun and the time of day therefore when the flocks and shepherds rested and all work came to a standstill, thus a period of *cauma* or 'calm'. This is also the origin of the French word *chômer*, 'to take time off work'.

JUBILEE

This is a word that has come down to us from Biblical times but has also changed its meaning somewhat in the process. We tend to use the word for those anniversary celebrations which have a special significance such as the twenty-fifth or fiftieth (silver and golden jubilees). But the original jubilees of the Old Testament were rather more solemn events, and their roots were firmly fixed in the Jewish calendar of feasts and festivals.

The Jewish system of festivals was based loosely on an almost mystical repetition of the number seven. The reason for this was the belief that God created the world in six days and on the seventh, the Sabbath, He rested. During the Feast of the Tabernacles, which was celebrated in autumn every year, people lived for seven days in crude shelters made from branches as a reminder of the time the Jews spent in the wilderness in tents. Then there was the custom of referring to every seventh year as a Sabbatical year. During this time, according to Mosaic law, the fields were to be left fallow and the people who would normally have been employed on the land were then required to study the word of God.

Immediately after the seventh such Sabbatical year (that is, every fiftieth) the land was left fallow for the extra year, and this was also declared a time when the land had to revert to its original owner. During this time also all those people who had not prospered and had suffered great hardship had their property (and freedom if they had been deprived of it) restored. Such a system was intended to ensure that people remembered that, ultimately, the land belongs to God. It was also a means of making sure that the rich did not acquire too much land and therefore power.

And the word 'jubilee' itself? This is derived from the Hebrew word *yobel*, which meant 'ram' and is a reference to the custom of signalling the start of a jubilee year by blowing several blasts on a ram's horn.

JUGGLER

From a historical point of view there is far more to juggling than the ability to keep three balls rotating through the air at any one time. A typical juggler was also expected to be something of an acrobat, a magician and, perhaps most importantly of all, a teller of tales.

The Latin infinitive *ioculari* meant 'to speak in a humorous manner', and its related noun *iocus* has given us our word 'joke'. Another derivative, *ioculator*, developed into the French word *jongleur*, the origin of 'juggler' in English. 'Joker' as an alternative to 'juggler' was a later development.

Another teller of tales in the Middle Ages was the 'jester', a word which in modern English always implies humour and funny stories. But this meaning did not apply before the seventeenth century. In the Middle Ages there were itinerant story-tellers who narrated the *chansons de geste*, long epic poems of derring-do, valiant knights and fair maidens in distress. The word *geste* was the French derivative of the Latin *gesta*, 'exploits', from the verb *gero, gerere, gessi, gestum*, 'to do', 'to perform'. The men who narrated these tales eventually became known as 'jesters'.

Other court entertainers were known as 'buffoons' and 'fools' and they share a strangely coincidental derivation. A buffoon was so called because part of his act was to puff out his cheeks and pull strange faces and grimaces, and the French word used to describe the act of making facial contortions was *bouffer*, 'to puff up'. No doubt this is also the origin of the 1960s' hair-style known as the 'bouffant'.

'Fool' has a similar derivation. The Latin word *follis* was originally a kind of leather bag, but it acquired the metaphorical meaning of a 'windbag' and then came to be applied to the court jesters who must have made quirky facial gesticulations as a standard part of their repertoire.

Another class of freelance entertainer of the Middle Ages were the *troubadours* and *trouvères*. These were professional poet–musicians who flourished in France in the twelfth and thirteenth centuries, the former plying their trade in the south of France and the latter entertaining in castles and at courts in the north. The origin of both terms is the verb *trouver*. In modern French this means 'to find', but in the Middle Ages it meant 'to compose' verse, music, etc. It appears that these versifiers would compose the material and then hire professional musicians known as 'minstrels' (from the Latin *minister*, 'a servant', 'a subordinate') to perform it in front of the lords and ladies.

But there is also another fascinating linguistic twist here. These *troubadours* or *trouvères* appear not to have enjoyed an entirely unsullied reputation, and their skill at invention seems not to have been confined to the performing arts. When they were not gainfully employed entertaining their lords and masters they must have resorted to begging in order to eat, and if this did not provide them with a full stomach they probably turned their hand to less lawful means of sustenance. We may safely assume this because another Old French word, also derived from the verb *trouver*, is *truand*, which meant either 'beggar' or 'crook'.

The concepts of both entertainer and crook come together in Spanish, where *truhán* means both 'rascal' and 'jester'. But the real surprise is both the Old French *truand* and Spanish *truhán* were adopted into English as 'truant', which originally meant 'an idler', 'a loafer'. It was not until the fifteenth century that the word was first applied to schoolboys failing to turn up for lessons.

KISS

There is some disagreement among etymologists about the derivation of this word. Some trace it back to the Greek word *kuneō*, 'to kiss' (which has a future form of *kusō*), whereas others maintain that it is connected with another Greek verb, *geuomai*, 'to taste'. Advocates of the latter theory point out that the letter 'g' changed to 'k' in German *küssen*, English 'kiss', but remained unaltered in French *goûter* and Spanish *gustar*, both of which retain the meaning 'to taste'. If 'to kiss' is related linguistically to the Greek verb *geuomai*, then both words have a common ancestor in the Indo-European root GUS, which is also the source of yet another English verb, 'to choose'.

LADY

This is one of those words which make the hairs on an etymologist's head stand on end. The simple word 'lady', when analysed for its linguistic provenance, leads over continents and back in time in a way which few words can, firing the imagination of anyone who can be enthralled at the discovery of unexpected etymological relationships and connections.

The Anglo-Saxon elements which go towards the formation of this word are *hláf* (loaf) and *daege* (kneader), the latter being directly related to the Gothic verb *digan*, 'to knead', 'to shape', 'to mould', and the modern English noun 'dough'. So the Anglo-Saxon noun *hlafdige*, which evolved into 'lady', denoted the lowly female servant whose responsibility it was to knead the dough and bake the bread. And when these household tasks had been performed, the man whose job it was to control the distribution of the finished product was none other than the *hláf ward*, the guardian of the bread, a title which eventually evolved into 'lord'.

The Gothic verb *digan* is allied to the English noun 'dyke' and can be traced all the way back to the Ancient Greek word *teikhos*, meaning 'wall'. The association here is not difficult to understand, as the most primitive walls would originally have been nothing more than earth moulded or shaped by hand in a manner reminiscent of kneading dough and shaping it into loaves.

Also cognate are the German *der Teig*, 'pastry', and the Russian *testo*, 'pastry', and the verb *tisnut*', 'to squeeze', 'to press'.

Now if we add the prefix *peri-*, 'around', to *teikhos* we form the Greek verb *periteikhizō*, 'to build a wall around', and its noun *periteikhos*, 'a surrounding wall'. This noun also appears in Old Persian in modified form as *pairidaeza*, and this subsequently found its way into English as 'paradise'. So the word 'paradise' really denotes nothing more than 'a piece of land surrounded by a wall'. And while on the subject of paradise we might as well point out that the parallel word in English, Eden, comes from the Hebrew *edhen*, 'delight', and the Greek *hedomai*, 'to enjoy oneself'.

The Greek word *teikhos* produced a compound *steikhos* (or *stikhos*) which was a term for a line of poles stuck in the ground and draped with netting to form a crude form of pen into which wild boars could be driven and then kept while awaiting slaughter. This word eventually found its way into Anglo-Saxon as *stigo*, a descendant of which is our word 'sty'. The man who tended the pigs in their pen

Further contraction of the word *apothēkē* involving the loss of the initial 'a' and voicing of the 'p' into 'b' produced the words *boutique*, the French for a little shop, and *bodega*, meaning a 'wine store' in Spanish.

What we refer to as an 'art gallery' is described in several European languages by another term which makes use of the Greek verb *tithēmi*. French has *pinacothèque*, Spanish has *pinacoteca* and German has *Pinakothek*. In all of these words *tithēmi* is combined with another Greek word *pinaks* which originally meant a slab or board and then came to refer to what was actually written, drawn or painted on it. Hence its association with art.

The use of the word 'gallery' in English to denote a room dedicated to the display of works of art only dates from the sixteenth century. Prior to that the word was applied to long covered walkways, possibly housing a collection of little shops, where people could stroll at their leisure. It was certainly always associated with pleasure or entertainment of one sort or another, as the word is derived from the Low Latin *galare*, 'to amuse oneself'. The association between a long walk and a gallery has led some etymologists to suggest that there could be a linguistic connection with the Middle High German verb *wallen* ('g' and 'w' interchange), meaning 'to go on a pilgrimage', with its modern German equivalent, *wallfahren*.

LICHGATE/LYCHGATE

A roofed gateway into a churchyard under which pallbearers can shelter from the rain while awaiting the arrival of the coffin. The word literally means 'corpse gate', from the Anglo-Saxon *lic*. The same word survives in modern German *die Leiche*, 'body', and the now archaic word for a graveyard, *der Leichenacker* (literally, 'corpse field').

The most interesting piece of etymology attached to this word is what happened to the Anglo-Saxon *lic*. Eventually it became the word 'like' in expressions such as 'king-like' and 'man-like', originally meaning 'having the body of a king or man'. This developed yet further until it became the suffix '-ly', giving us 'kingly', 'manly', 'earthly', etc.

LINGER

To linger over something means to take a long time over it, and the words 'linger' and 'long' are etymologically connected. Both are derived from the Greek *lagarizō*, 'to slacken', 'to make loose', and are cognate with the German *langsam*, 'slow', and other English words which convey the concept of sloth: 'laggard', 'lag'.

The Latin infinitive *languere*, a direct descendent of the Greek verb, meant 'to be faint', 'to be weak', and so conveyed the same idea of inertia and gave us the adjective 'languid' and the verb 'to languish'.

It has been suggested that the expression 'to long for' something or someone stems from the idea of inertia or anxiety being caused by the distance between oneself and the object of one's desires.

LUCRE

Now used as a deprecatory term for financial gain, as in the expression 'filthy lucre', the word has come down to us from the Latin *lucrum*, which was the normal word for 'profit' or 'gain' without any of the emotional overtones of the modern English word. The Latin word is connected with the Greek *leia*, meaning 'plunder' or 'booty', applied especially to stolen cattle.

It is also allied to the Irish word *luach*, 'price', 'wages', the German *der Lohn*, 'wages', 'reward', and the Russian verb *lovit'*, 'to attempt to catch'. The Indo-European root is LU, 'to gain', 'to acquire as spoil'.

MACHINE

When we think of the word 'machine' we invariably think of some industrial device, usually large, capable of doing the work of many people and thus releasing them from the drudgery of labour. The first machines, however, were military structures designed to intimidate, defeat and/or destroy an enemy.

The Greek word *mēkhanē*, from which 'machine' is derived,

meant nothing more than 'a device' or 'contrivance' for making difficult tasks easier. The associated verb *mēkhanaomai* meant 'to construct', 'to put together' either in a literal sense, and so could be applied to almost any process involving building or constructing, or it could be used figuratively to suggest the contrivance of plans, stratagems, wiles, etc. Hence our related English word with more negative connotations, 'machinations'.

The Indo-European root of *mēkhanē* is MAGH, 'to have power', 'to be strong', 'to be able'. This is the very same root that produced other words indicative of strength and ability such as the verbs 'might' and 'may' and the noun 'main' as in the expression 'with might and main'.

The same root appears also in other European languages. German, for example, has *Macht* for 'might' or 'power' and Russian has *moch'*, which as a noun means 'might' and as a verb 'to be able'.

MAFIA

The mafia (also known as Cosa Nostra, Italian for 'our business') is a criminal organization which began life as a gathering of Sicilian bandits who spread out from their small island and established themselves in the USA and then became one of America's chief exports to the rest of the world.

The word *mafia* is a Sicilian dialect word for 'bragging' or 'strutting' and was originally applied to the gang members on account of the brazen manner in which they flaunted themselves before the authorities. Ultimately, however, *mafia* is thought to be a corruption of the Latin Matthaeus or Matthew. The association here is with the Matthew in the Bible who, in his official capacity of tax-collector, spent his days demanding money from ordinary people before he became a disciple of Jesus.

MAWKISH

Since the eighteenth century this word has been used to indicate a certain sickly sentimentality or insipidness. Prior to that it was applied to almost anything unpleasant or nauseating, as the original meaning of the word was 'maggoty', derived as it was from the Middle English *mawk*, 'maggot'.

The immediate ancestor of *mawk* was the Old High German word *mado*, which could mean all of: moth, worm, insect, maggot. Its Latin and Greek cognates are, respectively, *mando, mandere, mandi, mansum* and *masaomai*, meaning 'to chew', which have also provided us with the words 'mandible' and 'masticate'.

MEAT

The sense in which this word is now used, that is to say to refer to edible animal flesh, dates from the fourteenth century. Prior to that the word meant food in general and still survives with this sense in expressions such as 'meat and drink' or 'one man's meat is another man's poison'.

Etymologists differ on the actual origins of the word, although there is some consensus that the Indo-European root is MAT, 'to measure', which would suggest that the original idea behind the word is that our 'meat' or food is a measured portion of that which we rely on to sustain our existence.

It is possible that the word is etymologically linked to the Sanskrit *medaš*, 'fat', and the Latin and Greek verbs *madere* and *madaō*, which both mean 'to be wet', 'to drip', the association here being with blood.

Assuming that this assumption is correct there is another etymological link for these Latin and Greek verbs are cognate with the words 'mast', an alternative word for fodder but especially the food of swine, and 'mastoid'. 'Mastoid', an adjective meaning 'shaped like the female breast', is derived from the verb *madaō* and cognate with *mastos*, 'breast', which has provided words such as 'mastitis', a medical term indicating inflammation of the breast. It is also cognate with the word Amazon, the term applied to the mythical women who are supposed to have cut off one breast (*a* = 'without' + *maston* = 'breast') in order to use a bow and arrows more effectively. It is also connected with the dinosaur known as the 'mastodon', so called because its molar teeth bore nipple-like protuberances.

MERRY

Etymologists differ about the origin of this word. All agree that it has come down to us from Anglo-Saxon *myrige* and Middle English *meri*, both of which meant 'pleasant' and 'joyful'. Some argue that it is cognate with the Old High German *murg*, meaning 'short' or 'brief', implying that merriment and jollity can never last for more than a brief time. At least one etymologist, C. Wyld, even suggests that it is possibly cognate with the Latin infinitive *marcere*, 'to shrink', 'to wither', but the reasoning here is not immediately obvious.

Walter Skeat, however, suggests that the origins might not be Germanic at all but Celtic and proposes a connection with the Irish noun *mire*, 'ardour', 'mirth', and the adjective *mireogach*, 'frolicsome', 'sportive'.

METAL

Referring to a substance that has to be dug out of the ground, this word has come down to us from the Latin *metallum*, meaning a 'mine' or 'quarry'. The Latin word itself was derived from an earlier Greek *metallon*, also meaning 'mine'. The derivation of this noun is the verb *metallaō*, 'to go in search of', from *meta alla*, which literally means 'after, in search of other things'. So a mine was to the Greeks a place where 'other things' could be sought below the surface of the earth in addition to those above it.

The idea of quest is reflected also in the Low Latin infinitive *minare*, 'to follow' (a seam of ore), and this has given us the words 'mine' and 'mineral'.

Russian also retains this concept of extraction in its word for mineral, *iskopaemoe*, a compound of *is* ('out of'), the root *kop-* ('dig') and a present participle passive suffix *-aemoe*. When all this is put together the literal meaning of the Russian is 'that which is dug out'.

METICULOUS

We now use this word only in a positive sense. If we say that somebody is a 'meticulous worker', for instance, we imply that he or she has excellent powers of concentration and that he or she pays

113

careful attention to detail. The origin of the word, however, was slightly more sinister.

The Latin word from which the modern adjective is derived is *metus*, 'fear', 'apprehension', 'dread', and is probably a reference to the days when extreme forms of punishment could be meted out to those whose work was not considered up to standard. The meaning of the original Latin is retained in a cognate word in Irish Gaelic, *meathach*, 'coward'.

MEWS

Since the seventeenth century this word has been used to designate stables arranged around a court or alley, the original being situated at Charing Cross in London in the first half of the sixteenth century.

Previous to this, however, the word 'mew' referred to the cages in which birds, particularly hawks, were kept while they were moulting. The word 'mew' itself came into English from French *muer*, 'to moult', which is a derivative of the Latin infinitive *mutare*, 'to change'. The linguistic association between 'to change' and ' to moult' is preserved in modern Spanish which has *mudar* with both meanings.

MIGRATE

'Migrate', 'immigrate' and 'emigrate' are all derived from the Latin infinitive *migrare*, 'to move from one place to another', and its associated noun *migratio*, 'change of abode'.

These Latin words, however, are descendents of the Greek verb *ameibō*, the basic meaning of which was 'to change'. Like its Latin counterpart this verb could also be used in the context of changing location but had many other meanings as well. It could mean 'exchange', 'recompense', 'repayment', 'barter' and 'alteration', and has provided us with the biological term for the microscopic life-form whose shape is constantly changing, the 'amoeba'.

Another word which the Greeks had for migration was *metabolē*. This word, too, could be used more generally to just mean 'change' or 'exchange', which is the origin of our term 'metabolism', the rate at which our bodies convert food into energy.

MOB

From the Latin expression *mobile vulgus*, a term used to describe the fickle common people. As an abbreviated form of *mobile* the word 'mob' is cognate with 'to move' and the Sanskrit *mív*, 'to push,' derived as they both are from the Indo-European root MU, 'to push'.

MONEY

The word 'money' has come into English from the Roman goddess Juno whose full title was Juno Moneta or Juno the Adviser. Her temple on the Capitoline Hill was where coins were produced, and this has given us another cognate word, 'mint'.

The root of the Latin word *moneta* is the infinitive *monere*, 'to advise', 'to warn', and reappears in words such as 'to admonish' and 'monster' which was originally something to be warned about. If we trace the roots back even further we see that, according to Skeat, the Latin verb itself is related linguistically to *mens*, meaning 'mind', and is thus the basis for such words as 'mental', 'mentality', etc.

Anyone who takes the time to look up the derivations of words associated with money soon realizes that there is a considerable overlap between financial matters and weights. The obvious correlation here is, of course, between the British pound sterling and a pound weight, and this is even more graphically illustrated when we consider that the 'L' of pre-decimal 'LSD' stood for *libra*, the Latin for 'scales'. Words such as 'pension', 'spending' and 'expenses' preserve the association with weighing as they are all derived from the Latin *pendo, pendere, pependi, pensum*, 'to weigh'. The basic concept here is that money was originally weighed out before distribution, and it would be difficult to find a better illustration of this than the Jewish shekel, which is derived from the verb *shaqal*, 'to weigh'.

If we consider what happened in Spanish-speaking countries where the peso and the peseta are used we find an interesting linguistic twist. *Peso* and *peseta* are nouns derived from the Spanish verb *pesar*, which means both 'to weigh' (transitive) and 'to be heavy' or 'to weigh' (intransitive). The Latin infinitive from which *pesar* is derived is *pensare*, which also gave *pensar*, 'to think' (French *penser*, Italian *pensare*), and the English adjective 'pensive'. Obviously the connection here is between 'weighing' something literally and figuratively. This is further supported by the difference in Latin between *pendere*, 'to weigh', and *pensare*, 'to weigh carefully'.

The 's' and 'd' elements of LSD stood for *solidus* and *denarius*, old Roman coins. The former has also given us the words 'solid' and 'soldier', the connection here being that a soldier was someone who hired out his military skills for 'hard cash'. A *dinarius* (whence the term 'dinar', still used as a unit of currency in many Mediterranean countries, and 'denier', the term used to denote the fineness of nylon, silk, etc.) was a Roman unit of currency roughly equal to the Greek *drachme*. This in turn originated in the word *dragma*, meaning a 'handful' and derived from the verb *drassomai*, 'to grasp'. It has also given us the word 'dram' for a unit of spirits.

Many countries, of course, use the term 'dollar' for their currency and in so doing hark back to the Europe of the Middle Ages. Its present spelling has evolved from the original German form *Thaler* which in turn is derived from the place-name Joachimst[h]al, 'Joachim's dale or valley', in what is now the Czech Republic, and referred to the silver mine there which produced the metal from which the coins were minted. The German Mark originated from the Anglo-Saxon *mearc*, a unit of weight for measuring silver, and the French franc is an abbreviated form of *Francorum Rex* (King of the Franks), inscribed on coins struck during the reign of Jean le Bon, ruler of the Franks from 1350 to 1364.

There is some disagreement about the origin of the good old English word 'penny'. It is known to be cognate with the German *Pfennig* and may also be related linguistically to the word 'pawn', which originally meant 'a pledge'. According to another theory the word is related to Penda, the Anglo-Saxon king of Mercia in the seventh century. The 'shilling', however, is probably from an Indo-European root SKIL, 'to divide', which in turn is associated with the root SKAR, 'to cut'. This may be a reference to the ancient practice of cutting individual coins out from a sheet of metal. If this is the origin of the word there is a direct parallel with the Russian word *rouble* as this is derived from the word *rubit'*, 'to cut'. The Russian *kopeck*, on the other hand, is from the Russian word *kop'yo*, 'lance'. The earliest kopecks were minted in the late fifteenth and early sixteenth centuries and bore an image of Ivan the Terrible (Ivan IV) wielding a lance, and this is thought to have given the coin its name.

The Russian *kop'yo* is related to the Greek words *kopis*, 'axe', 'cleaver', and *kopē*, 'cutting', 'slaughter'; both are derived from the verb *koptō*, 'to cut'. In other words 'rouble', 'kopeck' and possibly 'shilling' are all associated with cutting.

MOON

This word comes to us from the Greek *mēnē* and is cognate with the Sanskrit *masa*, 'a month'. Both are ultimately from the Indo-European root MA, 'to measure', the idea being that the moon is the measurer of time. Another Greek word for the moon is *selēnē*, which literally means 'brightness' and has given us the name Selina and the scientific study of the moon, 'selenology'.

The Latin word for moon, *luna*, has given us our word 'lunatic', as the ancients believed that a certain type of madness or lunacy was triggered by the full moon. Interestingly, however, a *lunátik* (stressed on the 'a') in Russian is someone who walks in his or her sleep.

MUCUS

From the Greek *mukos*, 'discharge', and the compound verb *apomussō*, from *apo*, 'away', and *mussō*, 'to wipe', meaning therefore 'to wipe away'.

If we follow the linguistic threads connected to this word, however, we make some fascinating discoveries. We also see how the discharge from the nose and the nose itself reminded the ancients of lamps, lamp-wicks and candles.

The Greek word *mukos* had a relative *muksa* which was an alternative word for 'mucus' but additionally also meant both a nostril and the nozzle (little nose) of a lamp. When *muksa* was adopted into Low Latin it became *myxus* but was now used to designate the wick that protruded from the nozzle rather than the nozzle itself. *Myxus* then made its way into French and Spanish where it appeared as *mèche* and *mecha* respectively, meaning 'wick' or 'fuse'. It then crossed the Channel, so to speak, and appeared in English as 'match', which originally meant the wick rather than the device used for setting fire to it.

The word 'snot', now considered vulgar, was a dialect form of 'snuff' until the fifteenth century when it acquired the meaning it has today. Both 'snuff' and 'snot' are related etymologically to 'snout' and the Anglo-Saxon verb *snyfan* (modern English 'sniff'), meaning 'to blow one's nose'.

The association between nasal excreta and illumination is further underlined by the German verb *schneuzen*, which used to mean 'to snuff out a candle' and now just means 'to blow one's nose'. And then there is the English custom of describing someone with a runny nose as having 'candles'.

MURDER

Technically speaking the legal definition of murder is the unlawful, premeditated killing of another human being.

English and German (which has *der Mord* with the same meaning) are unusual among European languages, the majority of which have words which repeat the consonant combination m-r-t (or the voiced equivalent, d) but which simply mean 'death'. Latin had *mors*, French has *mort*, Spanish *muerte*, Italian *morte* and Russian has *smert'*. For 'murder' Spanish has *asesinato*, Italian has *assessinio*, Russian has *ubiystvo*, whereas French comes closer to English and German with *meurtre*. The m-r-t/d combination can be traced back to the Sanskrit *mrta*, 'dead', the past participle of *mr*, 'die'.

Walter Skeat posits an interesting theory in connection with this Sanskrit root. He points out that *mr* is linked to the noun *maru*, 'desert', and takes his argument one step further by stating that linguistic descendants of the word can be seen in words for 'sea' in various European languages. The Latin *mare* spawned the French *mer*,

Spanish *mar*, Russian *móre*, Italian *mare* and German *Meer* as well as the archaic English word 'mere' for 'lake' which survives in place-names such as Windermere and Grasmere. Skeat goes on to explain the link between death and various words used to define expanses of water by pointing out that, to the ancients, the oceans of the world appeared like watery deserts and that, although they teemed with life beneath the surface, they themselves appeared lifeless.

Another cognate noun here is 'marsh'. The modern form of this word in English is derived from Anglo-Saxon *mersc*, an abbreviated form of *mer-isc*, literally meaning 'mere-ish', that is to say 'full of meres or pools'. An alternative to 'marsh' is a 'swamp', which is the same word etymologically speaking as 'sump' and related to the German *Sumpf* meaning 'pond'. The Greek word from which both the German and English words are derived is *somphos*, meaning 'porous', from another Greek word *poros*, meaning 'a way through'. The reference here is to the tiny passageways found in any porous material.

MYSTERY

The original mysteries were secret religious ceremonies associated with primitive cult religions in Ancient Greece. Gods such as Demeter and Dionysos, considered as wielding less authority than their Olympian counterparts, attracted followers who had to swear not to divulge details about the secret rites to anyone who had not been through the initiation ceremony. The Greek verbs involved here were *muō*, 'to be shut', especially when speaking of the eyes or lips, and *muaō*, 'to bite one's lips', that is, to remain silent. Both verbs were derived from *mu*, the sound that imitates most closely the murmuring noise we make when we try to say something with our lips tightly closed.

Some etymologists believe that there is a direct linguistic connection between this explanation of 'mystery' and the English expression 'to keep mum' about something.

n

NARCISSUS

Narcissus, in Greek mythology, was the son of Cephisus and Liriope. He was a beautiful youth who fell in love with his own image as reflected in the waters of a fountain and then pined away until he eventually changed into the flower of the same name. The idea of being in love with one's own image has given us the words 'narcissism', 'narcissistic', etc.

The Greek form of the word, *narkissos*, is etymologically linked to 'narcotic' because it used to be believed that the flower had narcotic properties and could induce drowsiness, stupor, contractions and cramp. The latter two words are a clue to the word's Indo-European root SNARK, 'to twist', 'to entwine', which is clearly seen in the verb *narkaō*, 'to grow numb', and the noun *narkē*, 'numbness'.

There is an interesting Modern Greek military meaning of *narkē*: an explosive mine, presumably from its ability to deprive victims of all feeling. And the Latin equivalent of *narkē* is *torpedo*, meaning either 'torpor', 'numbness' or the fish which we call the electric ray. Hence our military word 'torpedo', which is after all another kind of mine, can be said to have a direct linguistic association with the narcissus!

NEIGHBOUR

Literally, 'one who lives near'. The word is comprised of two Anglo-Saxon words, *neáh*, 'nigh', 'near', and *bur* or *gebur*, meaning 'tiller of the soil' or 'dweller'.

The reason for the wide difference in meaning between a 'tiller of the soil' and 'dweller' originates from the fact that the Indo-European root BHU had several meanings and gave rise over time to nouns and verbs with very dissimilar meanings despite their common ancestry. BHU had all of the following meanings: (i) to grow, (ii) to till the ground, (iii) to build and (iv) to dwell.

Associated with the first meaning, to grow, are verbs such as 'to become' and even 'to be', which is why the verb 'to be' is so similar in geographically dispersed languages such as the Russian *byt'*, Welsh *bod* and Irish Gaelic *bheidh*.

The English word 'boor', now used in the sense of a crude, uncultured person, was originally a 'tiller of the soil', and is allied to the Dutch *boer* (as in the 'Boer War') and German *Bauer*, meaning 'farmer'.

Bauen (not to be confused with *Bauer*) is the German for 'to build' and has its echoes in the English word 'bower' which was originally an inner apartment or dwelling place and only acquired its present-day meaning of an arbour in the sixteenth century.

The concepts of building and dwelling have here become a little confused, and the same lack of clarity is sustained when we realize that because of the common root the word 'neighbour' is linguistically liked with another English word, 'husband'. The word in Old Norse was *húsbóndi*, from *hús*, 'house', and *bóndi*, from *búa*, 'to dwell', so the original meaning of the word 'husband' was 'master of a household'. But in the thirteenth century the word was also used to mean a 'tiller of the soil', which gives us 'husbandman' as an alternative to farmer. And by the sixteenth century the word had acquired yet another meaning – 'one who manages' – which is why we also have the expression of 'animal husbandry'.

NIB

This is the part of a pen which makes contact with the paper to produce writing as it is moved across the page. The Anglo-Saxon word from which it is derived was *nebb*, but this had nothing at all to do with writing implements and actually meant a bird's bill or beak.

The adoption of the word *nebb* or 'nib' to refer to the tip of a pen may be due to nothing more than the similarity of form between the point of a pen and a beak. On the other hand, there is a far more romantic explanation with its roots in the ancient world of the Pharaohs.

Legend has it that the ancient Egyptians believed that writing as a technical skill was invented by their moon-god Thoth, reputed to be the patron of scribes. His representative on earth was the ibis, a wading bird related to the stork and treated in Egypt as sacred.

According to the legend, the ibis spent much of its time writing mystical signs with its long curved beak in the mud along the banks of the Nile.

NICE

This word has changed in meaning beyond all recognition. It is now applied to almost anything considered pleasant, so that we talk of having a 'nice' time, we can say that so-and-so is a 'nice' person or talk about a 'nice' distinction when we mean a 'subtle' or 'fine' one.

When the word entered English in the thirteenth century, however, it meant only one thing: stupid. It was adopted from the Latin adjective *nescius*, which in turn was derived from *ne*, 'not', and the verb *scio, scire, scivi, scitum*, 'to know'. This is the same verb, in fact, from which we derive the word 'science' (Latin *scientia*), which simply means 'knowledge'.

The connection between ignorance and 'niceness' is probably explained by the ancient belief that congenital idiots were especially blessed by God.

NIGHT

Nearly all European languages possess words cognate with 'night' to describe the hours of darkness. German has *Nacht*, French has *nuit*, Spanish *noche*, Russian *noch'* and Irish Gaelic *oiche*, to name but a few. All can be traced back through Sanskrit *nashta*, meaning 'dead', 'lost' or 'invisible', to the Indo-European root NAK, 'to be lost', 'to perish'. It is also cognate with the Latin infinitive *necare*, 'to kill', and the Greek adjective *nekros*, meaning 'dead'.

The association between night, death and lost time is reflected in Greek mythology where death (*thanatos*) and sleep (*hupnos*) were represented as being twins.

NIGHTMARE

This word has absolutely nothing to do with female horses. The 'mare' element of the word is from the Anglo-Saxon word *mara*, meaning a weight, the reference being to a feeling of something or someone crushing the person as he or she sleeps. Other languages also express the idea by reference to heavy weights; for instance, Spanish has *pesadilla* (from *pesar*, 'to weigh', 'to be heavy') while French and Russian preserve the *mara* in *cauchemar* and *koshmar* respectively. The Italian *incubo* echoes the idea of an 'incubus' or evil spirit which was thought to visit sleepers and cause bad dreams. The Latin verb from which 'incubus' and *incubo* are derived is *incubo, incubare, incubui, incubitum*, 'to lie heavily on', which also gives us our verb 'to incubate'.

The German for 'nightmare' is *Alptraum*, which at first sight seems to suggest a heavy weight (the Alps) sitting on one's chest and preventing normal breathing. In fact the word is comprised of two elements, *Alp*, a 'demon' (cognate with the words 'elf' and 'oaf' in English) thought responsible for nightmares, and *Traum*, 'dream'.

NOMAD

The original nomads were tribes that moved around with their herds and flocks constantly in search of pasture lands. The Greek for such people was *hoi nomades*, a term coined from *nomós*, 'pasture' (not to be confused with *nómos*, 'law'), and the verb *nemō*, 'to drive to pasture'.

There is an additional interesting linguistic link here. The verb *nemō* also meant 'to dwell', 'to hold', etc., and 'to deal out', 'to distribute'. The last meaning is etymologically related to the concept of Nemesis, the Greek Goddess of Divine Retribution. It was her role, as the Greeks saw it, to 'distribute' punishment to those who had become excessively vain.

NOON

Now a synonym for midday, the original meaning of 'noon' was 3 p.m.

The word is derived from the Latin phrase *nona hora*, meaning 'ninth hour', that is, the ninth hour after what was considered the beginning of the day, 6 a.m. It seems that the tradition was for monks to break off for a meal at the 'ninth hour', but the pangs of hunger moved the meal back further and further until everyone stopped for a break at midday. In the twelfth century the Latin *nona* was being used for the midday meal, and then in the thirteenth century it became a term applied to the time of day rather than the meal itself.

NYMPH

This is a complicated one. We now use this word either with reference to sprites such as water-nymphs or to describe beautiful young girls. To the Ancient Greeks a *numphē* was a marriageable young woman or young bride and the word was derived from the verb *numpheuō*, 'to give a daughter away in marriage'. The stem of this verb, *numph-*, is etymologically linked to the Latin verb *nubere*, meaning 'to marry' or 'to be married to'. But *nubere* also meant 'to cover', the connection between the two meanings obviously being the custom then as now of draping a bride's face with a veil. The derivative adjective and noun *nubilis*, 'nubile', and *nuptiae*, 'nuptials', are also directly linked to *nubes*, 'cloud', the association here being between the veil which covers the bride's face and the fluffy masses that hide the sun from view.

A Greek word related to the Latin *nubes* was *nephos*, 'a bank of cloud', and this found its way into Russian as *nebo*, but changed its meaning on the way to 'sky'. But then *sky* was the Old Norse for 'cloud' and our word 'cloud' came from the Anglo-Saxon *clúd* which originally meant 'a pile of rocks'. The Anglo-Saxon for what we refer to as a 'cloud' was *weolcen* (archaic English 'welkin', the sky) which is cognate with modern German for cloud, *Wolke*.

OBITUARY

Used in modern English to mean the announcement of a death rather than the death itself, this word has come to us via Old French *obit*, 'funeral rite', from Latin *obitus*, 'death', 'downfall', 'setting' (of the sun, moon, etc.). The Latin verb from which it is derived is *obeo, obire, obivi, obitum*, made up of the verb *ire*, 'to go', and the prefix *ob-*, 'down'. The basic concept behind the verb, therefore, is 'going down' in more of a metaphorical than a literal sense. However, as this verb was also used in Latin to mean 'go to meet' it is just possible that the underlying idea was that death is merely the beginning of a journey we all take in order to meet another world, other souls, others who have died before us.

ODD

This has to be one of the 'oddest' words in the whole of the English language and one that causes considerable trouble for the foreign student of the language. Consider, for instance, the following uses:

(a) The numbers 3, 5, 7, etc., are called 'odd' numbers (they are not divisible by 2).

(b) 'He's very odd' (strange).

(c) 'This book cost 40-odd pounds' (that is, a little bit more than £40).

(d) 'This is an odd shoe' (for the other one of the pair is missing).

(e) 'At odd moments I like to just sit and think' (when I have nothing else to do).

(f) 'He went out of the house wearing odd socks' (they were not matching).

(g) 'His homework contained the odd mistake' (the mistakes were few and far between).

Then there is the even more obscure and confusingly subtle difference contained in the sentences 'I paid twenty odd pounds for this vase,' and 'I paid twenty pounds odd for this vase.' In the first example I paid an unspecified amount but certainly more than £21 for the vase. In the second I paid more than £20 but less than £21 for it.

How did all these meanings come about? Believe it or not, they all stemmed from the Old Norse word *oddi*, which meant 'triangle'. The basic idea was that any triangle by its very nature consisted of two points and a third 'odd' one, and this idea of the one which was not part of the greater group eventually produced the whole gamut of meanings we now have in modern English.

But there was a further development of meaning in Old Norse. Because the 'odd' point was almost invariably the tip of the triangle it came to be associated with the sharp end of a spear, which in Old Norse was the *oddr*. This eventually came to be applied to strips of land if they were triangular in shape and then to any piece of land whether it was of triangular shape or not. This association with territory is seen in the modern German cognate noun *Ort*, meaning 'place'.

ODEON

A favourite name for cinemas during their heyday, the original *ōdeion* was a public building built by Pericles (*c.* 495–429 BC) in Athens. Its main function was as a place of musical entertainment (although it also doubled up as a court of law), as can be seen from the root of the word, *ōdē*, 'song'.

The Greek *ōdē* is obviously the derivation of the word 'ode' in English, although it has changed its meaning from 'song' to 'poem' and as such has lost its associations with musical accompaniment.

On the other hand, when we use the word 'rhapsody' we usually imply the involvement of music. But the original Greek term *rhapsōdia* had several meanings, all of which were allied to poetry rather than song. It could simply mean the recitation of epic poetry, or in a metaphorical sense it could be applied somewhat disparagingly to a rambling story which was beginning to bore those obliged to listen to it. But it was also used to denote sections of epic poetry considered suitable for recitation at a single sitting such as a book of the *Iliad* or *Odyssey*. There were, in Ancient Greece, groups of people who eked out a living by doing nothing more than give public recitations of the works of Homer. Such people were know as *rhapsōdoi*.

What was the origin of the word? We have already seen that the Greek word *ōdē* meant 'song'. The interesting thing here, however, is that in its plural form *ōdai* the meaning changed to 'lyric poetry'. The *rhaps-* element is from the Greek verb *rhaptō*, 'to sew', 'to stitch', so the real meaning of the word 'rhapsody' is 'stitching songs or poems together'.

OFFAL

We now use this term to denote the less expensive parts of the animal being sold as meat, particularly the entrails. The word originally referred to the parts to be thrown away and came into English from the Dutch *afval* and is cognate with the German *Abfall*, 'garbage', 'rubbish', 'stuff to be thrown out'.

OSTRACIZE

Ostracism was the Ancient Greeks' version of 'blackballing'. If someone was to be banished from Athens for misdemeanour, the matter was put to a vote and if enough people wrote the name of the person in question on an *ostrakon* or potsherd then the ostracism was put into effect.

Ostrakon was derived from *osteon*, which meant 'oyster' or 'oyster shell', and this in turn was from *osteon*, 'bone', 'shell'. And *osteon*, from *ásthi*, the Sanskrit for 'bone', appears in medical terms such as 'osteoarthritis' (inflammation of the bone joints), 'osteoporosis' (lack of bone density), etc.

p

PANIC

We now use this as a noun or verb, but strictly speaking it is a Greek adjective, as in the expression to *panikon deima* (Pan fear, that is, fear induced by Pan). In Greek mythology Pan was an important Arcadian god whose cult was spread throughout Greece by the orgiastic festivals in honour of Dionysos, the god of wine, vineyards and dramatic poetry.

Legend has it that Pan was one of Zeus' most faithful attendants and that, during the battle between the Gods and the Titans, he let out such blood-curdling screams that he caused the giants to flee in fear or, in other words, to 'panic'.

PANTRY

Modern English now uses this word to designate a cupboard used for storing food in general, but its origins lie in the Latin word *panis*, meaning 'bread'. It came into English via Old French which had developed the word *paneterie* from the Low Latin *panetaria* or *panitaria*, which was the word for a place where bread was either made or kept. The Low Latin words were from the Latin *panarium*, meaning a 'bread basket'.

The concept of companionship is also related to these words. 'Company', for instance, is derived from the Low Latin *companies*, a compound noun formed from *cum*, 'with', and *panis*, 'bread', which originally was a word used to define the custom of eating bread together. 'To accompany', therefore, originally meant 'to eat bread with', and a 'companion' was the person with whom the bread was shared.

Russian has an interesting parallel here. A colloquial Russian word for a close friend is a *sobutyl'nik*, which is made up from *so-*, 'with', *butyl'*, a (large) bottle, and the noun suffix *-nik*. So, to the Russian mind, a close friend is more likely to be somebody with whom you have shared a bottle (presumably of vodka!) rather than someone with whom you have eaten a loaf of bread.

Another word which has a very similar meaning to 'pantry' in English is 'larder'. Any food can now be stored in a larder, but originally it was not a room at all but just a tub in which bacon fat was stored. The Old French word for this tub was *lardier* which was derived from the Latin *lardum*, 'bacon fat' or 'lard'. This in turn was derived from the Greek *larinos*, an adjective meaning 'fatted' or 'fat' and itself linked etymologically to another adjective, *laros*, meaning 'sweet' or 'tasty'.

PARASITE

Two Greek words have combined here, *para*, 'alongside', and *sitos*, 'corn', 'grain', 'food', to produce another noun *parasitos*, which was used to describe somebody who ate at another's table. It seems to have been a regular feature of daily life in Ancient Greece to have people join the richer members of society at table, and in return they would entertain and/or flatter their hosts. As the word found its way into Latin as *parasitus* it acquired the meaning of both a guest and a toady.

PAWNBROKER

This is a dealer in 'pawns' or 'pledges', from the Old High German word *Pfant* and cognate with the modern German *Pfand*, meaning a 'pledge', 'security' or 'deposit'. The modern German equivalent of a 'pawnshop', for instance, is a *Pfandhaus*, and *gegen Pfand* is a sign seen everywhere in Germany informing the populace that a deposit has to be paid for the use, hire or purchase of certain articles.

The Lombards were the people who established pawnbroking in England in the thirteenth century, and the three balls they used as their insignia are still in use today. These balls are thought to have been copied from the coat of arms of the Medici family in honour of Averado de' Medici. He is reputed to have served as an army commander under Charlemagne and to have slain a giant, bringing home as a trophy the giant's club which was adorned with three balls.

The other explanation that the three balls represent odds of two to one against getting your money back is probably folk etymology.

The Lombards also provided English with the word 'lumber'. We now think of a lumber room as one in which infrequently used articles are kept, but originally it was a 'Lombard room', that is, the place where Lombardeers (an old term for pawnbrokers) stored their pledges.

PAY

As both a noun and a verb this word is derived from the Latin *pax,* 'peace', and the infinitive *pacare*, 'to placate', 'to appease'. Such appeasement involved the offer of money or an acceptable substitute which would suffice to keep the workers quiet.

'Remuneration' is from the Latin infinitive *remunare*, 'to repay', a compound verb formed from the infinitive *munerare*, the basis of which is the noun *munus*, meaning 'gift' or 'reward'.

'Stipend' is from the Latin *stipendium*, which either meant 'tax', 'contribution', or was the term used for a soldier's pay. The root of this was *stips*, a small coin originally used as a religious offering. There may be a connection here with the English modern use of the word which tends to be used when referring to clergymen's salaries.

'Emolument' is thought by most etymologists to have its origins in the Latin verb *molo, molere, molui, molitum*, 'to grind'. The word came into English from the Latin *emolumentum*, 'effort', 'gain', 'advantage', but originally referred to the money paid to a miller by a farmer in exchange for grinding his corn. The Latin infinitive *molere* has also given rise to the words associated with grinding corn in many European languages: English 'mill', Spanish *molina*, French *moulin*, German *Mühle* and Russian *mel'nitsa*. It is also, therefore, cognate with the term for the large teeth used for grinding food, the 'molars'.

The more normal words in use in modern English to denote reward for labour are 'salary' and 'wages', words not without a certain flavour of class distinction. The so-called 'white-collar' workers normally receive a 'salary', a word derived from the Latin *salarium*, which originally meant nothing more than 'money to buy a salt ration with' (from *sal*, 'salt'). 'Wage', on the other hand, is the Anglo-Norman form of *gage*, meaning 'pledge'.

PERIOD

We now think of a 'period' exclusively as an expression of time, but the Greek word from which it is derived had closer associations with space.

The components of the word are *peri*, 'around', and *hodos*, 'way', 'road', 'journey', so the original Greek *periodos* meant 'going around', 'travelling about'. By association with movement *periodos* acquired the following additional meanings: (i) a book or account of travels abroad, (ii) a chart or map, (iii) the orbit of a heavenly body. Later it acquired the meaning of 'a cycle of years' and then came to mean any length of time as in modern English. Interestingly, the same process of evolution has taken place in Greek, as the modern word retains only the temporal meaning.

The Greek noun *hodos* is more common in English than most of us realize. It crops up in several words, combined with different prefixes and sometimes in a disguised form, frequently in use in English.

A 'method', for instance, is a particular approach to a given task. The Greek elements here are *meta*, 'after', 'following', and *hodos*, 'road', so a 'method' is really just 'the road to follow' or the 'way' we go about getting things done. If we replace the prefix *meta* with *eks*, 'out of', we get *eksodos*, 'way out', although we more usually use the Latinized form of the spelling, 'exodus'.

If we turn to the world of science we see further examples of *hodos* in conjunction with various prefixes. The word 'anode', for instance, is made up from the Greek *ana*, 'up', and *hodos*, giving a literal meaning of 'the way up', and a 'cathode' is from the Greek *kata*, 'down', and *hodos*, and thus means 'the way down'. A 'diode' is from *dis*, 'twice', plus *hodos*, a reference to the two electrodes in a thermionic valve or the two terminals in a semiconductor rectifier.

The Greek noun *hodos* was derived from the verb *hodeuō*, 'to travel', 'to wander', 'to go'. But Greek also had another verb (although it was only used in the future tense) for 'to go', namely *eimi*, and an examination of these two verbs and comparison of them with other European languages reveals some surprises. For a start the root vowel of *eimi* is the letter I, and this shows itself clearly in the plural of the verb paradigm: *imen*, 'we will go', etc. If we compare this with languages such as French, Spanish and Latin we see that this letter I recurs time and time again in verbs of motion and nouns derived from them. French, for example, has *aller* as the infinitive, but the future is *j'irai, il ira, nous irons*, etc. Spanish has the letter I in the infinitive *ir* as well as in the future *iré, irás, irá* and the imperfect *iba, ibas, iba*. The Latin verb 'to go' has the principal parts: *eo, ire, ivi, itum*, and this verb has spawned many words in modern English such as 'itinerary', 'itinerant', 'ambient' and even the word 'ambition'. Anyone with 'ambition' was originally someone who wanted to get on in the world of public affairs and so went around canvassing for votes and asking people for their support. According to Skeat, the same Indo-European root, I, lies at the base of the word 'year', a word cognate with the Sanskrit *yatu*, the literal meaning of which is 'that which passes'.

Another Greek noun derived from *eimi* is *isthmos*. This has been absorbed into English, although Latinized into 'isthmus', as the term for a narrow strip of land surrounded by water. *Isthmos* is related to another noun derived from *eimi*, namely *ithma*, 'a step', 'movement'. The important thing about these nouns is that they may not only be linked to but may also explain one of the most characteristic features of the Slavonic languages, namely the verbs of motion. Russian, as an example, distinguishes between unidirectional motion and non-unidirectional motion, and has two basic verbs to distinguish between the two. So *Misha khodit po parku* (unspecified direction) would mean 'Mike is walking about in the park', but *Misha idët v park* (specified direction) translates as 'Mike is walking to the park'. Russian has the verbs *khodit'* and *idti*, which are related to the Greek *hodeuō* and *eimi* (notice the recurrent

I in the Greek *eimi* and Russian *idët*, third person singular of the infinitive *idti*).

The question now is this: could the Greek concept of walking in a straight line as along an isthmus be the genesis of the Slavonic unidirectional and non-unidirectional verbs? After all, walking along an isthmus almost always has to be in a straight line.

PETARD

This word now really only survives in the expression 'to be hoist on one's own petard' meaning to be caught in a trap one has set for others, but the literal meaning is 'to be blown up by one's own bomb'. A petard was originally a small bomb designed to blow holes in walls or blow doors in. The word is derived from the Latin *pedo, pedere, pepedi* and the Greek *perdomai*, both of which meant 'to break wind' and are closely connected etymologically with our word 'to fart'. It is a good example of the Indo-European p/f interchange.

Cognate words survive in other modern European languages such as French which has *péter*, 'to fart', and now uses *pétard* for an explosive firework – 'a banger'. *Péter* also features in the vulgar but graphic expressions *Il veut péter plus haut que son cul*, 'He tries to appear better than he is' (literally: He wants to fart higher than his arse), and *Je l'ai envoyé péter*, 'I told him to bugger off.'

Russian also has *perdet*, 'to fart'.

PETITION

The Latin verb from which 'petition' is derived had many meanings. *Peto, petere, petivi, petitum* could mean (i) 'to make for', 'to head for', (ii) 'to attack', 'to assail', (iii) 'to strive for', 'seek to attain', (iv) 'to fetch', 'to derive', and, finally, (v) 'to ask for', 'to beg', 'to beseech', 'to request', 'to entreat'. The common denominator here is the idea of approaching an object (another cognate noun is 'impetus') or person. Sometimes the approach is hostile and sometimes not, which is why the verb covers the whole gamut of meanings from an outright physical attack to a mere request.

The Indo-European root from which *peto* is derived is PAT, 'to fly'. This root is also the linguistic ancestor of the Greek *petomai*, 'to fly', and the nouns *potē*, 'flight', *pteron*, 'feather', and *pteruks*, 'wing'. Another cognate noun is the Latin *penna*, which emerged in English as both 'feather' (Indo-European p/f interchange) and 'pen' as a writing implement.

PHALANX

Loosely used now to denote almost any large group of people assembled together for a single purpose, this word has changed its meaning considerably over the centuries.

As a battle formation it was used to great effect by the Ancient Greeks and then borrowed enthusiastically by the Romans. For the Greeks the phalanx was a densely packed group of infantrymen (usually eight men deep but sometimes as many as twenty-five) which, as a tactical formation on the battlefield, was learned by Philip of Macedon from the Theban general Epaminondas.

The word did, however, have other meanings, the original one being 'a block of wood', 'a tree-trunk' or 'a log'. No doubt the association here with the battle formation was due to fact that both convey the impression of density.

The link between the two meanings of the word is probably another Greek noun *phallos*. This meant either 'penis' (probably more recognizable in its Latin form *phallus*) or the wooden imitation of a penis which was carried aloft at Bacchic festivals to symbolize fertility and the reproductive abilities of Nature. So close, in fact, was the association in the Greek mind between the *membrum virilis* and a tree-trunk that the associated adjective *phallinos* simply meant 'wooden'.

Related nouns in other European languages include Latin *palus*, German *Pfahl* and Russian *palka*, all of which have the same meaning as and are cognate with the English nouns 'pale' and 'pole'.

PLAGIARIZE

'To plagiarize' has been used to mean stealing somebody else's literary work since the eighteenth century. Originally, however, its use was far from literary, as it has come down to us from the Latin word *plagiarius*, meaning 'a kidnapper'. This word in turn was linked to *plaga*, a net used in hunting and basically designed for catching animals, but presumably it could be used with a human prey also.

The idea of 'kidnapping', 'stealing', etc., was a direct result of the original Greek word from which the Latin words were derived. *Plagioō* means 'I move sideways' and is associated with the adjective *plagios*, 'placed sideways', 'slanting', 'at an angle'. Used metaphorically, *plagios* acquired the meaning of 'treacherous', 'underhand', and this is the concept that gave us our present usage.

POLICY

This word has two very unrelated meanings for the simple reason that their origins have become confused. 'Policy' as a course of action is from the Greek word *polis* which is usually translated as a 'city state' and has given us derivatives such as 'police' and 'politics'. So 'policy' originally referred to the decisions adopted by those in government or at least in a position of authority. The Greek *polis* can be traced back to the Sanskrit *purí*, 'a town', which itself is derived from the Indo-European root PAR, 'crowded', 'full'.

According to Skeat the word 'policy' as an insurance document is really nothing more than a piece of paper which is so long that it has to be folded several times in order to reduce it to a manageable size. The Greek word from which our word is taken was *poluptukhon*, from *polu,* 'many', and *ptuks*, 'a fold'. The noun *ptuks* is from the verb *ptussō*, 'to fold up'.

However, there is some disagreement concerning the etymology of this word and other linguists see it as a corruption of the Late Latin *apodissa*, itself a corruption of the Greek *apodeixis*, 'showing', 'proof', from the verb *apodeiknumi*, 'to show', 'to demonstrate'.

Coincidentally the word 'diploma' has a similar origin. Its root is the Greek word *diplos*, 'twice', and is derived directly from the verb *diploō*, meaning 'to fold in two'. So a 'diplomat' is someone who holds a folded document or 'diploma' which allows him or her certain privileges.

POLLEN

The curse of all hay-fever sufferers, the word 'pollen' has now been taken over by the scientific fraternity to denote the minute particles discharged by flowers for the purposes of reproduction. But the Latin word *pollen* meant 'fine flour' or 'meal', which was a borrowing from the Greek *palē*, 'sifted meal'. This was from the verb *pallō*, which could mean almost anything to do with violent movements of the arms. It meant 'to brandish', 'to swing', 'to toss', and was even used to describe the convulsions of a fish flapping about on dry land. It must also have been used to describe the action of sifting flour vigorously, hence its association with fine dust-like particles.

PORNOGRAPHY

Literally 'writing about or drawing prostitutes'. The Greek words forming the basis of this word are *graphō*, 'to write or draw', and *pornē*, 'prostitute'. *Pornē* comes from the verb *porneuomai*, 'to sell oneself', 'to become a harlot', a verb which itself is a derivative of *peraō*, which meant 'to sell and export for slavery'. The connection is the fact that many females sold abroad in those days were forced into prostitution by their new masters.

The Latin word *fornix* meant a 'vault' or 'arch'. As certain arches or arcades in the seedier parts of Rome became the haunts of prostitutes plying their trade, *fornix* acquired the additional meaning of 'brothel', and the result was a certain linguistic confusion. The adjective *fornicatus* originally meant nothing more than 'arched', but it came to be applied mainly to the area where the sex trade was conducted, and so eventually the English verb 'to fornicate' evolved; it must originally have meant 'to behave like those women who ply their trade under the arches'.

It is tempting to postulate a connection here between the Greek and Latin words on the basis of the Indo-European p/f interchange. But this would mean that the Greek base verb *peraō* made its way into Latin and reappeared as the word for an arch. This seems highly unlikely, so the association between the Greek and Latin nouns is purely coincidental.

PORT AND STARBOARD

The port side of a boat or ship is on the left-hand side as seen by an observer looking towards the bow.

Originally the left-hand side of a boat was known as the 'larboard', but this word was too easily confused with the word 'starboard', particularly when high winds made it difficult to hear what someone was saying if they were standing more than a few feet away. So 'larboard' became 'port' purely for reasons of convenience and safety.

The word 'starboard' is from the Anglo-Saxon *steor*, 'rudder' (hence modern English 'steer'), and recalls a time when the steering mechanism, including the rudder, was on one side of a boat rather than astern as is the custom today. 'Larboard' is thought to be derived from the word *laddeborde*, which was the Anglo-Saxon term for that side of the boat used for loading goods from the shore or dockside.

PRECARIOUS

An actor's life is often described as a 'precarious existence' because he or she can never be sure when, or indeed if, their next role will come along. A vase can be 'precariously' balanced on the edge of a table if it appears to an observer that it is about to topple over. In other words, any situation can be described as precarious if it is unsafe, unsure or depending on pure chance or the luck of the draw.

The original Latin word *precarius*, however, meant 'obtained by prayer' and was linguistically connected with the noun *prex*, 'prayer', and the deponent verb *precor*, *precari*, 'to pray', and these in turn are cognate with the German *fragen*, 'to ask' (Indo-European p/f interchange).

The use of the word in English to mean 'depending on chance' dates from the seventeenth century.

PREVARICATE

We accuse someone of prevarication when he or she refuses to give anything more than a non-committal answer. English acquired this verb from the Roman legal system, whereas *praevaricator* was an advocate who had entered into some kind of secret arrangement with his client's opponents and was therefore indulging in what modern slang would term 'double-crossing'.

The base of *praevaricator* was *varus*, an adjective which could mean 'bent', 'knock-kneed' or 'crooked', either literally or figuratively. A further relative was the deponent verb *praevaricor, praevaricari*, which retained both a literal and figurative meaning in that it could mean 'to walk with an irregular gait' or 'to be guilty of collusion'. But closest in meaning to the modern English verb are the adjectives *varicus*, which meant 'straddling' (think of the expression 'sitting on the fence'), and yet another verb *varico, varicare*, 'to stand with one's legs apart'.

There is, however, an even more fascinating etymological association. Because of the confusion between the various literal and metaphorical meanings and the overall connotations of distortion, another noun appeared in Latin, *varix*, which had the same meaning for the Romans as does the modern English medical term derived from it, 'varicose veins'.

PSALM

The Book of Psalms in the Old Testament is a collection of songs intended specifically for accompaniment by the harp. The Greek derivative noun is *psalmos*, from the verb *psallō*, which basically meant 'to touch' but was also used to show that a stringed instrument was being played by having the strings plucked as opposed to being struck with a *plectrum* (the Latin form of the Greek word *plēktron*, from *plēssē*, 'to strike'). In time the verb acquired the additional meaning of 'to sing to a harp accompaniment'.

Psallō is thought to be cognate with the Latin *palpo, palpare*, 'to stroke', 'to caress', and this verb is known to be cognate with the Russian noun *palets*, 'a finger'. The noun *palets* in turn is cognate with the Greek *palamē*, which can mean either the blade of an oar or the palm of the hand and is in turn cognate with Anglo-Saxon *folm*, 'hand', and the verb *felan*, the modern English verb 'to feel'. *Folm* has given us our word 'fumble'.

PSYCHIATRIST

Unlike a psychologist, who merely studies how the mind works, a psychiatrist attempts to cure it when it ceases to function normally.

The first syllable of this word is a direct borrowing of the Greek *psukhē*, meaning 'mind' or 'soul'. But the verb from which it is derived is *psukhō*, 'to blow', 'to breathe', which reflects the degree to which in ancient times a person's soul and their breath were thought to be at least closely connected if not actually one and the same phenomenon. Indeed, even in modern times there persists an assumed association between the two as is attested by everyday metaphorical expressions such as 'to draw breath' and its opposite 'to breathe one's last'.

The second part of the word is derived from the Greek word *iatros*, 'doctor', 'healer', and the verb *iaomai* ,'to heal', 'to cure'. Interestingly, however, the derivation can be traced further back to an earlier verb *iainō*, 'to warm', which by Homer's time had acquired the additional meaning of 'to cheer' in the sense of to make somebody feel better. It is not unreasonable to deduce from this that in ancient times a basic medical technique involved nothing more than keeping the patient warm.

The Indo-European root contained within the verb *iainō* is IS, 'to move swiftly', 'to be vigorous'. Presumably the linguistic and physiological thread here connects warmth, well-being and movement. No athlete, for instance, would attempt serious physical exercise without a preparatory 'warm-up', and, at the other end of the scale, do we not associate death (that is, total lack of movement) with cold?

Warmth, then, is a sign of life. We associate it also with active emotional responses, so that if we say that someone is 'warm' we generally intend the description to be a positive one, unlike our description of a 'cold fish' who might be capable of 'cold-blooded murder'. If we notch up the temperature and say that, for instance, the Italians and Spanish are 'hot-blooded' we imply that they are easily roused to passionate responses which may indicate either sexual eagerness or just a fiery temper. The Latin for such wrath was *ira*, another word directly descended from the Indo-European root IS and the origin of the English word 'ire'.

Yet another word derived from the root IS was the Greek *oima*, a noun which could be applied to any impetuous attack, although its particular application was to such attacks as a lion's leap or the deadly swoop of an eagle on to its prey. Directly related to this word was the term for one of the ever-present pests with which the Ancient Greeks had to contend, the gadfly (thought to be a corruption of goadfly) for which the Greek term was *oistros*. But *oistros* was not only applied to the infuriating little insect but also to the smarting pain and possibly uncontrollable frenzy that resulted from its sting. This word, retaining both meanings, passed into Latin as *oestrus*, the scientific term now used in English to denote a period of sexual arousal. Combined with the suffix *-gen* (birth, origin, source) *oestrus* becomes 'oestrogen' (that which generates sexual frenzy), the term invented by biologists to denote the steroid hormones responsible for the development of female characteristics in mammals.

PUDDING

Now usually thought of as something sweet with which to finish a meal, the original puddings were animals' stomachs, crammed with fillings of one sort or another and usually including meat, which resembled the modern sausage. This meaning still survives in the delicacy known as 'black pudding'.

Although its immediate antecedent is thought to be the Old French *boudin*, there seems to be little doubt that the word is of Celtic origin, and various forms of it can still be detected in the Celtic languages: Welsh has *poten*, meaning both 'pudding' and 'paunch', Irish Gaelic has *putóg*, and Cornish, a language that died out in the eighteenth century, had *pot* for a 'bag' or 'pudding'. All of these can be traced back to the Indo-European root PUT, 'to swell'.

The Irish *putóg* has a plural form *na putóga*, meaning 'intestines', which features in a wonderfully graphic expression used to describe the darkest months of winter: *putóga dubha na bliadhna*, 'the black entrails of the year'.

PUMPKIN

This form of the word only appeared in English in the seventeenth century. Previously the word had been 'pumpion' and had arrived in English, via Latin and French, from the Greek word *pepōn*. This could be used either as a noun, in which case it denoted a large melon, or as an adjective with the meaning of 'ripe'.

Both as an adjective and a noun the word *pepōn* was derived from the verb *peptō*, which had several meanings. Basically it meant 'to make something soft' and, when applied to the action of the sun, 'to ripen'. By extension it came to be associated with almost any process involving the conversion of basic foodstuffs into edible form so that, depending on the context, it could mean 'to cook', 'to boil' or 'to bake'. When applied to the activities of the stomach it even acquired the meaning 'to digest' and is therefore related to such words as 'peptic' and 'dyspepsia', the medical term for indigestion.

PYTHON

Since the sixteenth century this word has been used to designate the genus of snake that kills its prey by constriction and asphyxiation.

The name is derived from the Greek myth according to which Apollo killed an enormous serpent at Delphi, the seat of the famous oracle, close to which was the port of Phocis which had formerly been known as Puthō. Because of the close association between Delphi and the port, both were frequently referred to by the older name of Puthō, and the serpent acquired its name from the geographical location.

The apparent female to the male python, pythoness, is just that, apparent. The word does not denote a female snake but means a 'witch', 'sorceress', 'female seer'. This is in fact an alternative name for the female soothsayer who lived at Puthō/Delphi and is more commonly known as the Delphic Oracle.

Apollo is thought by some to have acquired his name from the legend of how he slew the great serpent at Delphi, since the name appears linked etymologically with the Greek verb *apollumi*, 'to destroy', 'to slay'.

QUAFF

With the meaning of 'to drink in large quantities', 'quaff' is a borrowing of the Scots and Irish Gaelic word *cuach*, which simply means a 'drinking cup' or 'goblet'. The change of spelling from 'ch' to 'ff' is merely a reflection of the English inability to reproduce the Gaelic guttural sound 'ch' which is probably best known to *Sassanachs* (from the Gaelic for 'Saxons') from the Scots for 'lake', *loch*.

A word of similar meaning is the verb 'carouse'. Until the sixteenth century the word had been used as an adverb in expressions such as 'to drink carouse' meaning to drink to the dregs, but with time it came to be used as a verb in its own right. The reason for the earlier adverbial usage is explained by the fact that the word was derived from a German phrase *gar aus*, where *gar* means 'completely' and *aus* is has a colloquial meaning of 'finished', 'over'. The expression 'to drink carouse' therefore was a literal translation of *trinken gar aus* and meant 'to drink till there's nothing left'.

The verb 'to booze' (and its associated noun 'boozer' which can either be applied to the person who likes a drink or three or the establishment where alcoholic beverages are dispensed) is from the Dutch verb *buizen*, 'to drink too much'. This verb is derived from the noun *buis*, meaning 'a pipe' or 'tube' and, by extension, the tap on a barrel.

r

READY

This is a short, insignificant-looking word but one with an interesting history. It is derived from the Anglo-Saxon verb *rídan*, 'to ride' or 'to go on a raid'. The adjective originally meant 'equipped to go riding' or 'equipped to go out on a raid'. It is also directly related to another derivative, the word 'road', which originally meant 'that which one rides along'.

REEK

The verb 'to reek' is now used in English almost exclusively with negative connotations. It is associated with particular unpleasant smells as when we say that someone 'reeks of beer' or that a room 'reeks of stale cigar smoke'. Formerly, however, it meant to 'give off smoke' and is therefore cognate with German *rauchen*, as in *rauchen verboten*, 'smoking forbidden', and its derivative *räuchen*, to smoke food as in *Räucherschinken*, 'smoked ham'. It is also directly related to the Icelandic capital Reykjavik, which means 'smoky inlet', and the affectionate name the inhabitants of Edinburgh bestow on their fair city, 'Auld Reekie' ('Old Smoky'). We hear it again in the traditional Scots benediction 'Lang may yer lum reek,' that is, 'Long may your chimney produce smoke.' This is a roundabout way of expressing the hope that the person being addressed will always be able to afford to keep warm.

The association with smell as opposed to the mere production of smoke is preserved in another German cognate verb, *riechen*. But the German verb can have pleasant as well as unpleasant connotations, so that it is possible to say both *das riecht gut*, 'that smells good', and *es riecht schlecht*, 'there's a bad smell here'.

Etymologically the word 'reek' is related to the Anglo-Saxon *rec*, 'vapour', the Latin infinitive *eructare* and the Greek *ereugomai*, both of which mean 'to belch forth', 'to vomit', 'to throw up', and are thus additionally related to the noun 'eructation', the more learned word for belching.

The English word 'smoke' is from the Greek *smukhō*, which meant 'to burn slowly', 'to smoulder'. But one of the Greek nouns for 'smoke' was *tuphos*, a noun which had the secondary meaning of 'cloud' and is cognate with the English word 'dust'. Figuratively it was also used to describe the high temperature and delirium associated with fevers and so gave us the medical term 'typhus'.

RELUCTANT

Since the eighteenth century the word 'reluctant' has meant nothing stronger than 'unwilling'. If, for instance, I say that I am 'reluctant' to do something it does not mean that I definitely will not do it but suggests that compliance will be less than wholehearted. Prior to the eighteenth century it implied resistance and even definite refusal, and this meaning was closer to the original Latin verb from which it is derived, although closer examination of the history of the word reveals a strange reversal.

The Latin derivative verb is *reluctor*, *reluctari*, 'to wrestle against' (a compound verb formed from the basic *luctari*, 'to wrestle'), which explains the basic idea of the word as it is used in English. A reluctant bride struggles against a proposed marriage.

However, the original Greek word which lies at the root of both the Latin verb and the English adjective is *lugos*, a noun which denoted any pliable, flexible twig, particularly the willow. Eventually the noun *lugos* developed into a verb *lugizō*, 'to bend', 'to twist', and then it came to be applied to the sport of wrestling in which it acquired a specific meaning of 'to throw an opponent'. So the flexibility of the willow provided a wrestling term and then the inherent idea of resistance passed into Latin and ultimately English.

The same Greek words, *lugos* and *lugizō*, also found their way into other languages and produced linguistic cousins which come as something of a surprise. For instance, they reappeared again as the Old Norse noun *lokkr*, and this found its way into Anglo-Saxon as *locc*, which is our word 'lock' as in a 'lock of hair'. The association here is the same flexibility and pliability found in the Greek wrestling manoeuvres.

REVEAL

To reveal something is to uncover it, to take the wraps off, to bring out into the daylight. The base noun here is the Latin *velum*, which meant a cloth or veil and combined with the prefix *re-*, 'back', to produce an infinitive revelare which meant 'to draw back the veil'.

However, *velum* had an older, more specific meaning of a 'sail', derived from the verb *veho, vehere, vexi, vectum*, 'to pull', 'to drag along'. The obvious connection here is the sail as a source of power which propelled sailing ships over the water. The same verb produced a dry-land equivalent of the sailing ship, namely a *vehiculum* or carriage, and this has given us our word 'vehicle'.

RISK

Etymologists differ over the origin of this word, but Skeat confidently opines that the word has come into English from Latin via Spanish and that its closest relative is the Spanish word *risco*, meaning 'a steep rockface'. *Risco* is derived from the Latin infinitive *resecare*, 'to cut back', 'to cut off short', and thus gives the impression of a cliff edge which appears to have been sliced away from the main rock formation in such a way as to make any approach to the edge extremely perilous. In other words, anyone who ventures close to such a geological feature is 'taking a risk'.

RIVER

One of the early Greek philosophers stated that a river only exists by virtue of its banks. At the time he probably did not realize how, centuries later, western European languages would support his theory, for English and French define a river not by reference to the flowing water but to the land on either side. The Latin word *ripa* means 'bank' (hence the adjective 'riparian'), and this evolved into 'river' in English and *rivière* in French.

The Latin *ad ripam* meant 'to the bank' or 'to the shore', and

145

when travellers in the ancient world reached the end of a sea voyage they said that they had come *ad ripam*. This evolved into the English 'to arrive', a verb which only acquired its later meaning of reaching any destination (by sea or land) in the fourteenth century.

ROBOT

This is a twentieth-century borrowing into English from Czech and is applied to automated machines that do the work which otherwise would be done by people. In Czech *robota* means 'forced labour'. The same word appears in Russian as *rabota*, the general word for 'work', and both the Czech and Russian forms are linguistically connected to the German *Arbeit*.

Also cognate is the Russian word *rab*, meaning 'slave', which is derived from the Latin *orpus* and Greek *orphanos*, both of which mean 'orphan'. The connection between a slave and an orphan is explained by the custom of taking in orphaned children to act as unpaid skivvies.

Yet further cognates are the German words *der Erbe*, 'heir', and *das Erbe*, 'inheritance'.

RODENT

From the Latin word *rodo, rodere, rosi, rosum*, meaning 'to gnaw', 'rodent' is cognate with other words such as 'corrode' and 'erode', all of which retain the same basic meaning of eating away.

It may seem a far cry from the idea of gnawing, but the word 'rostrum' is a linguistic cousin of 'rodent'. The explanation lies in the fact that the original 'rostrum' was a pulpit or speakers' platform in the Forum in ancient Rome decorated with the prows of the enemy ships which had been captured at the Battle of Antium (modern Anzio) in 338 BC. The Latin word *rostrum* had a basic meaning of 'beak' or 'snout' (as the prow of a ship was by analogy) and literally meant 'that which gnaws'.

The Indo-European root RAD, 'to split', 'to gnaw', 'to scratch', from which *rodere* is derived, also spawned the Sanskrit *rada*, 'tooth', and Low Latin *ratus*, which turned up in English as 'rat'.

Another member of the rodent family, the mouse, has a very different linguistic history. Most European languages have very similar words for this tiny creature: Anglo-Saxon had *mús*, Russian has *mysh'*, Greek had *mus* and German has *Maus*. The Indo-European root for all of these is MUS, 'to steal', so the original meaning of the word is 'an animal that steals'. The Latin for 'mouse' was *mus* and its diminutive form, *musculum*, 'a little mouse', gave us the word 'muscle' because muscles were thought to resemble mice when they moved.

Two exceptions here are French and Spanish. The former has *le souris* for 'mouse', and the latter has *la rata* for 'rat' and *el ratón* for 'mouse'. Confusingly, the Italian word for 'mouse' is *topo*, which in Spanish means 'a mole'.

ROYAL

The word 'royal', together with associated words such as 'regal' and 'regent', has come down to us from the Latin word for king, *rex*. This in turn has its origins in the Indo-European root RAG, meaning 'to stretch', 'to make straight' and hence 'to rule'. The same root has given us the words 'reign' and 'right' and reappears in other languages such as in the German word *Reich*, Hindi *raj* and *rajah* and is even the origin of the suffix '-ric' in 'bishopric'.

The root RAG also can be seen in the Greek verb *oregō*, 'to reach', 'to straighten', 'to stretch', associated in the Greek mind with straightening oneself out and tensing one's muscles in readiness to do battle. Hence the derivative noun *orgē*, 'anger', 'passion', and a further verb *orgaō*, which meant both 'to swell with moisture' and 'to be on heat' (of animals) and also, as Liddell and Scott delicately put it, 'of men, to swell with lust'. This linguistic progression has given us our word 'orgasm'.

The same Indo-European root also gave us the word 'rich' which was originally applied to powerful, influential people with the means and property to command deference and respect.

RUBBISH/RUBBLE

These are connected with the verb 'to reave', an old English word meaning 'to steal', 'to plunder', and the German *rauben*, 'to rob'. Surprisingly it has also given us our word 'robe' as an article of clothing but which originally meant booty, particularly anything worn by a dead soldier of which he could be 'robbed'.

S

SABOTAGE

An act of sabotage is designed to hinder the enemy's progress, disrupt their plans and generally inflict casualties on them in time of war.

The root of the word is the French *sabot*, meaning a wooden clog. The derivation of the word itself is unknown, and all that can be said about its association with deliberately caused damage is that it is used in several French expressions denoting sloppy workmanship, inefficiency and carelessness. The noun *sabot*, for instance, in addition to denoting an article of footwear, can denote a sloppy worker or, when applied to a boat, a 'rust bucket' and a 'clapped-out old banger' when applied to a car. The verb *saboter* means 'to mess things up', 'to botch up a job', etc.

It has been suggested that 'sabotage' might be a reference to the practice of throwing a clog into a piece of machinery to put it out of action, but this is only a theory and has yet to be verified, but there is a linguistic echo which seems to lend weight to this suggestion. We do, after all, talk about something 'clogging up the works' when things go wrong.

SACK

To the Greeks *sakkos* (or *sakos*) could mean any of: coarse cloth made from horsehair; anything made out of such material and therefore bags and sacks; a sieve or strainer; a shaggy beard. The

Greeks almost certainly borrowed the word from the Hebrew *saq*, meaning either sack-cloth or a sack designed especially for the transportation of corn.

There is no definitive explanation of our use of the expression 'to give someone the sack' when we are referring to an employee's termination of employment. Most explanations, however, revolve around the idea that a hired workman, who may have been provided with accommodation by his employer, would be handed his bag of belongings and told to leave the premises. The earliest known reference to such a practice seems to be the French expression, current in the seventeenth century, *donner à quelqu'un son sac et ses quilles*, which translates literally as 'to give someone his sack and skittles'. This expression was apparently applied to servants who had been dismissed 'bag and baggage' by their masters. The significance of the skittles, however, remains obscure.

When we talk about 'the sacking of Rome' we enter the territory of disputed etymologies once again. Some etymologists maintain that the verb 'to sack' in this context is nothing more than an extension of the noun and that 'sacking' a town simply refers to the act of carrying away booty in sacks. Others, however, see the word as an abbreviation of 'to ransack', which is derived from the Old Norse *rannsaka*. This verb is comprised of two elements, *rann*, 'house', 'dwelling', and *saekja*, 'to seek', so the verb itself means 'to search a house' for anything thought to be worth stealing.

SARDONIC

This adjective is usually applied to laughter to mean 'scornful' or 'sneering'. The origin of the word is thought to be the Greek *sardonios*, from the noun *sardonion*, a plant which grows profusely in Sardinia (Greek Sardo). Tradition has it that this plant is so bitter that it makes anyone who eats it screw up their face.

SCANDAL

Now associated with shocking behaviour and moral indiscretions, this word originally meant 'a trap for an enemy'. The Greek word was *skandalon*, which itself was derived from *skandalēthron*, the stick on which the bait was placed and which sprung the trap when touched. Both words derive from the verb *skandalizō*, 'to trip somebody up'. Eventually the word assumed the figurative, metaphorical meaning of behaviour causing the downfall of someone caught misbehaving.

SCAVENGER

Now an uncomplimentary term of contempt, if not abuse, a 'scavager' (the 'n' was a later addition) was an official in the Middle Ages who performed two vital roles. Originally he was tasked with collecting taxes from foreign merchants who wished to display their wares and thus had to pay 'scavage' (Anglo-Saxon *sceawian*, 'to look at', 'to display'). Later on he was also expected to supervise the cleaning of the streets where the markets were held, and it is this association with the rubbish that others had discarded which has given the word its modern connotations.

SCHOOL

It may come as a bit of a shock but the word 'school', which we associate with hard work, 'swotting' (a corruption of the word 'sweating') and the nerve-racking, inexorable approach of examinations, comes from the Greek word *skholē*, which originally meant 'leisure' and 'spare time'. Later it came to refer to the informed discussions and debates conducted during such free time, and later still to the places where such discussions took place.

The original Academy took its name from Akadēmos, a Greek hero who is said to have planted the olive grove and gardens where Plato (429–347 BC) encouraged his students to engage in articulate discourse and philosophical discussion. Some of these students went on to form a group of philosophers known as the Academics, and their 'Academy' survived until it was dissolved by Emperor Justinian in AD 529.

Another garden in Athens, this time the one where Aristotle 384–322 BC) taught, has given us the word 'lyceum' (from the

Greek word *lukeion*), a grand term for a place of learning (adapted by the French into *lycée*) and ultimately derived from the Greek word *lukos*, meaning 'wolf'. This rather surprising association stems from the fact that the garden in question was close to the temple of Apollo who was frequently referred to as Apollōn Lukeios ('Apollo the Wolf-like' or 'Apollo of the Wolves') because he was associated with the daylight and the early dawn greyness which reminded the Ancient Greeks of the colour of a wolf's coat.

We cannot be certain, but there may be a parallel here with the Louvre art gallery in Paris. It has been suggested that the former palace was built on forest land which had been the home of packs of wolves (*loup* is the French for 'wolf'). Another suggestion is that the area was not so much the home of packs of wolves but one of the city's red-light areas. The connection here is the word *lupara*, which is not only thought to be the original name of the palace but also the Latin for 'she-wolf' with a secondary meaning of 'prostitute'.

'College' and 'university' share similar histories in that they both came to mean 'guild' or 'society' and originally referred to any group of people brought together by common interests. 'College' is from the Latin *con* (with) and *legere* (to gather). The same roots give us the word 'colleague'. 'University', like 'universe', is from *unus* (one) and *vertere* (to turn), originally meaning 'everything turned into one', 'all considered together'. This later produced *universitas magistrorum et scholarium* or the 'union of teachers and scholars' but was soon abbreviated to 'university'.

One of the most interesting educational derivations is that associated with the word 'gymnasium'. The root of the word is the Greek *gumnos*, meaning 'naked', and is a direct reference to the Greek practice of conducting all sporting activity in the buff. English, Spanish and French all use forms of 'gymnasium' to designate places where physical training takes place, but the equivalent words in German and Russian (*Gymnasium* and *gimnazia*) are used to describe what in Britain would be termed a 'grammar school'. Interestingly, however, the Swiss bridge the gap by using the French word *gymnase* with the German meaning of a grammar school.

When the grammar schools were founded in the sixteenth century their teaching concentrated on Latin and Greek, Literature and Philosophy. They took their name from the Greek word *gramma*, with the original meaning of 'a letter of the alphabet' (from *graphō*, 'to write'), which later developed into what we now understand as 'grammar', the rules governing the structure of language. The comprehensive schools which have largely replaced the old grammars take their name from the Latin infinitive *comprehendere*, meaning 'to grasp' or 'to include'. Only the most cynical of etymologists would point out that the same Latin root also gave us the word 'prison'!

When we consider institutions such as technical colleges and colleges of art the linguistic waters get very muddy. These two types of educational establishment conjure up very different images to our modern minds, but the fact is that, from a linguistic point of view, there is very little difference between them. 'Technology' is from the Greek *tekhnē*, which meant 'art' or 'craft' (the word 'architect' for instance was originally *arkhi-* + *tekton*, meaning 'chief carpenter'). 'Art' comes directly from the Latin *ars*, which also originally meant 'skill', 'way', 'method'. This in turn is from an older Greek verb *arariskō*, meaning 'to join together', 'to fasten' or 'to fix', all of which sounds to us more 'technical' than 'arty'. On the other hand, the technical sense of the verb is more evident in Russian derivatives such as *soorudit'*, 'to construct', and *orudie*, which originally meant 'an implement' but now means 'an artillery piece'.

In the UK the various periods of instruction into which the day is divided are known by different names depending on the status of the teaching institution. In a university professors and lecturers deliver lectures and conduct seminars and tutorials, whereas in schools teachers take classes or lessons, and all of these terms have interesting origins. 'Lecture', 'lecturer' and 'lesson' are all derived from the Latin *legere*, 'to read' (its other meaning of 'to gather' has already been mentioned). 'Seminar' is from the Latin *seminarium*, meaning a 'seedbed', the implication being that the lecturer should show the seeds of learning in students' minds. 'Tutor' and 'tutorial' are from the Latin *tuor, tueri*, 'to protect', as a tutor's role originally was to guard, not instruct. A 'professor' was originally someone who had declared his religious affiliations in public (Latin *profiteri*, 'to avow') and the term was first applied to the head of a university department in the fourteenth century.

Universities are populated by 'students' (from the Latin *studere*, 'to be busy', 'to be zealous'), and schools are divided into 'classes' made up of 'pupils' under the guidance of a 'teacher'. Originally a 'class' (Latin *classis*) was a group of people who had been summoned together (Latin *calo*, 'I summon'), and the word 'pupil' is derived from the Latin *pupillus*, 'an orphan', which in turn is derived from *pupus*, which simply meant 'boy'. Not until the sixteenth century did the word acquire its present meaning.

'Teacher' has come down to us from the Anglo-Saxon verb *taecan*, which meant 'to show', 'to demonstrate how to do something', and is thus also allied to the Greek verb *deiknumi*, 'to show'. This in turn is derived from the Indo-European root DAK, 'to teach', 'to show', whence we also derive words such as 'doctor' and 'docile'. The former passed into English from the Latin *doctus*, meaning 'taught', and the latter from *docilis*, 'capable of being taught'.

SCONE

The original scones were round flat cakes made of heat or barley and baked on a griddle so that they resembled what are now more usually referred to as pancakes or griddle scones. Their first appearance in England is thought to have been around the sixteenth century when they were introduced from Holland, where they were known as *schoonbrot*, literally meaning 'beautiful bread'.

The origin of the adjective *schoon* is the Old High German *sconi*, which meant both 'bright' and 'beautiful' and is cognate with the modern German for beautiful, *schön*, and also with the English 'sheen'.

The connection between scones and the noun 'sheen' is due to the slight lustre present on these delicacies when perfectly baked.

153

SEASON

We now use this word to refer to almost any period of time ('the season of good will', 'the mating season', 'the cricket season', etc.), but the derivation of the word betrays the fact that it was originally applied only to springtime. Spring was the most important period of the year to primitive societies, as it was the time when seeds and crops had to be planted, and it is this annual activity that has generated the word. The Greek verb *hiēmi*, 'to release', 'to let fly', was used to describe the action of 'casting' the seed over the soil, and the same verb appeared in Latin as *sero, serere, sevi, satum*, 'to sow', 'to plant'. The Indo-European root here is SA, 'to cast', 'to scatter', which can also be detected in words such as 'seed', 'semen' and the Russian *seyat'*, 'to sow'. Another similar Indo-European root SPAR, 'to sprinkle', produced the Greek verb *speirō*, 'to scatter', which generated words now used in English such as 'sporadic', 'spore', 'sperm', 'sparse' and 'diaspora'. And before leaving *hiēmi* we should perhaps also mention that one of its compounds, *eniēmi*, 'to throw in', 'to send in', is the origin of the medical term 'enema'.

If we look at the names of all four seasons of the year we find that some are more easily explained than others. With 'spring' there is no difficulty at all. The word simply denotes that time of year when plants begin to grow and 'spring to life'. But a glance at a few other languages throws up some interesting little snippets. The French *printemps* is derived from the Latin *primus*, 'first', plus *tempus*, meaning 'time', and *tempus* itself is from the Greek *temnō*, 'to cut', and thus suggests a portion or 'slice' of time. The evidence for *tempus* meaning either time in general or a period of time is seen in the expressions *tempus est*, 'it is time to', and *anni tempora*, 'times' or 'seasons of the year'. Spanish *primavera* is the Latin for 'the beginning of spring' (*primus*, 'first', and *ver*, 'spring' in Latin), and the German *Frühling* is derived from *früh*, meaning 'early'.

'Summer' is related to the Sanskrit *samayah*, which meant 'occasion', 'time', 'season', and another word *sama*, 'year' or 'half a year'. There is an interesting linguistic echo here in the relationship or confusion between 'year' and 'summer' in Sanskrit. The Russian words *god* and *leto* mean 'year' and 'summer' respectively. But the normal genitive plural of *god* is *let*, which is really the genitive plural of *leto*, so a Russian will talk about *dva goda*, 'two years', but *pyat' let*, 'five years' (Russian requires the genitive singular after numbers 2, 3 and 4 but genitive plural from 5 to 20).

The languages of northern Europe (the Germanic and Scandinavian) all have words relating to and resembling the English 'summer' for this time of the year, whereas the Romance languages have taken their words from the Latin and Greek. French has *été*, Spanish has both *estío* and *verano* (from *veranum*), which are descended from Latin *aestas*, and this in turn is from the Greek *aithō*, 'to light up', 'to kindle', and is associated with the verb *therō*, 'to heat up'. The latter verb also produced the Greek for summer, *theros*, which is at the root of other words in English associated with heat, such as 'thermos', 'thermo-nuclear' and 'thermometer'.

'Autumn' is something of a mystery. The word only came into general use after the sixteenth century, before which time the word 'harvest' referred to the time of year rather than the agricultural activity. Some authorities maintain that the word is derived from the Latin *augeo*, *augere*, *auxi*, *auctum*, 'to grow', but the obvious problem here is that autumn is the season when growth stops and plants prepare for the winter. It is just possible that the connection is not with plants at all but with the nights 'growing' longer, although this is only supposition.

Another suggestion, and one which sounds eminently plausible, links the prefix 'aut-' with the Gothic prefix *aud-* in the word *audags*, 'happy', 'rich'' and the Anglo-Saxon *eadig*, 'prosperous'. If this is correct then the word 'autumn' probably describes that time of year when an abundance of food engendered feelings of contentment and prosperity.

The term 'fall' is now used only in American English, but there was a time when it was the normal word to describe the time of year in UK English, too, and the word does have a certain resonance with languages such as Serbo-Croat, on the one hand, which uses *listopad* (literally 'leaf fall') for October and Polish and Czech, on the other, which, somewhat confusingly, have the same word but apply it to the month we call November.

There seems to be little doubt or disagreement among etymologists about the word 'winter'. It means 'rainy season' and is cognate with the words 'water' and 'wet', the Greek *hudōr* and the Russian *voda* and even the English word 'otter'.

English also converts the noun 'winter' into a verb 'to winter', so that such a sentence as 'they always winter in the Yorkshire Dales' is now considered perfectly acceptable. But when we are referring to animals sleeping through the winter months we prefer the more scientific-sounding description of their 'hibernation' from the Latin word for winter, *hiems*. *Hiems* was a Latin borrowing of the Greek *kheimōn* and its associated word *kheima*, 'wintry weather', 'cold', 'frost'. The Greek terms are linguistically connected with Sanskrit *hima*, 'frost', 'snow', as in the 'snowy mountains' or Himalayas. The same Sanskrit word also shows up in the Russian word for winter, *zimá*, and the Greek for snow, *khiōn*, which is thought to be derived from the verb *kheō*, 'to pour'.

SEDUCE

Now used to mean to persuade someone to do something against their will, the original Latin meaning of the verb was 'to lead away'. The figurative meaning of 'to lead astray' was a later development, and the sexual connotations we now tend to attribute to the word date only from the sixteenth century. Until the fifteenth its meaning in English was to persuade someone to change allegiance.

The Latin word was *seducere*, a compound made up of *duco, ducere, duxi, ductum*, 'to lead', and the prefix *se-* (*sed-* before vowels), denoting separation. This prefix is found in other words now current in English such as 'secure' (literally 'away from care, danger'), 'sedition' (literally 'going away') and 'separate', which really means 'to set apart'. The prefix *se-* is itself a contraction of *sui*, the genitive of *suus*, 'his', 'her', 'one's own', which suggests that the literal meaning of the verb 'seduce' is 'to lead astray for selfish reasons'.

SHAMBLES

Originally this word meant a 'butcher's slaughterhouse', and then it was used metaphorically to describe scenes of carnage on the battlefield. Still later it acquired the meaning which we now attach to it, of general or total disorder.

The word comes from the Latin *scamellum* or 'bench' on which the meat sellers would place the carcasses while they chopped them into smaller more manageable chunks. *Scamellum* is related to the Greek verb *skēptō*, 'to support', 'to prop up', which produced another noun, *skēptron*. For the Ancient Greeks this was just a walking stick, but it has given us our symbol of monarchy and imperial authority, the 'sceptre'.

SHARK

Etymologists differ on the origin of this word, and fall into two groups. There are those who simply state that the derivation cannot be stated with confidence, and those who, like Skeat, believe that the word is a corruption of the Greek *karkharos*, meaning 'sharp-pointed', 'jagged' and, tellingly, 'having sharp teeth'. The fact that the Greeks also had the word *karkharias* which applied to a large fish with sharp teeth lends weight to Skeat's argument.

'Shark' is also thought to be the derivation of the verb 'to shirk', meaning to avoid work, loiter, prowl or, generally, to scavenge.

SHILLELAGH

This is a good example of how etymologists differ in their opinions of the origin of a word. Several authoritative dictionaries tell us that this word denotes a kind of cudgel used in Ireland and named after the village of Shillelagh in County Wicklow. Some also take the definition further and say that the village and the cudgel both take their name from the fact that the particular part of Ireland is famed for its oaks and blackthorn. The most authoritative of the Irish dictionaries, edited by Patrick Dinneen, however, gives a very different etymology.

For a start, the word 'shillelagh' is a corruption of the Irish Gaelic *sail eille*, where *sail* is basically a willow tree but is also used metaphorically for anything strong and hefty and thus is a fitting epithet for a stout cudgel. The word *eille* is the genitive of the noun *iall*, which means 'leash' or 'thong' and specifically the thong attached to a cudgel. So, strictly speaking, a *sail eille* or 'shillelagh' is simply a cudgel with a thong attached to it.

Secondly, the association with oaks and blackthorn is rather difficult to explain, as the Irish for an 'oak' is *dair* (its derivative *doire*, 'oak grove', accounts for the suffix '-derry' in place-names such as Londonderry) and a 'blackthorn' is *draighean* (or *draighean dubh*). But there is a particular type of shillelagh, made out of blackthorn instead of willow, and known as a *maide* ('stick') *draighin duibh* ('of blackthorn').

SHINGLES

This word denotes a medical complaint usually characterized by a painful rash which frequently appears on the midriff ('mid' and Anglo-Saxon *hrif*, 'belly') and then gradually creeps around the whole waist area. The word 'shingles' is a corruption of the Latin *cingulus*, 'a belt', from the verb *cingo, cingere, cinxi, cinctum*, 'to surround'.

The medical term for 'shingles' is 'herpes', which is a direct borrowing from the Greek *herpō*, 'to creep', 'to crawl'. The verb *herpō*, when it was adopted into Latin, changed into *serpo* and produced the noun *serpens*, which is our word 'serpent'.

SHOP

A good old Anglo-Saxon word – almost! Its closest ancestor is the Anglo-Saxon word *sceoppa*, meaning a stall or booth. It is allied linguistically to *scypen*, another Anglo-Saxon word meaning a pen for keeping cattle in and as such is directly related to the dialect word 'shippon', used for 'cowshed' in the north of England. But even here we cannot get away from Ancient Greek roots, because 'shop' can be traced back to the noun *skepas*, 'a cover', and its associated verb *skepazō*, 'to shield', as well as the word *skia*, which gives us the words 'shade' and 'shadow'. The same Greek word is also at the root of our word 'squirrel', derived as it is from *skia* (shadow) and *oura* (tail).

The story does not end there. The Indo-European root here is SKU, 'to cover' (allied to SKA, 'to cover', 'to shade', 'to hide'), and this can easily be identified in the Latin word *scutum*, 'a shield'. This in turn produced *scutarius*, 'a shield-bearer', which eventually found its way into French as *escuyer* and gave us the word 'squire'.

And as an illustration of just how far words can spread out we should also mention that the Irish Gaelic for 'shield' is *sciath*, which is the Greek for 'shade' adapted to fit in with Irish orthography.

SHOPLIFTER

It would be easy to think of this word as meaning someone who 'lifts' things from shops, but not so. 'Lifter' comes from the Gothic *hlifan*, 'to steal', and *hliftus*, 'a thief'. It is cognate with Latin *clepo, clepere, clepsi, cleptum*, 'to steal', and the Greek word for a rogue or thief, *kleptēs*, which also gives us the medical term for the compulsion to steal, 'kleptomania'.

SHROVETIDE

'Tide' is the old word for 'time' and 'shrove' is allied to the word 'shrift', meaning 'confession'. The term came into being in the fifteenth century and was applied to the days leading up to Lent when people were obliged to confess their sins in church and pay a penance. A written record of all penances was kept, hence the term 'shrift' from the Anglo-Saxon *scrífan*, 'to impose a penance', which is cognate with the Latin and German verbs *scribo, scribere, scripsi, scriptum* and *schreiben*, 'to write'.

When we talk about giving someone 'short shrift' we are really referring to the brief time granted to a condemned man in his cell to make his confession to a priest before receiving the 'prescribed' punishment for his crime.

SINCERE

There are two possible, and very different, explanations for the origin of this adjective.

The simpler of the two is that the Latin word *sincerus* ('pure', 'uncontaminated') is a compound of *sine*, 'without', and *cera*, 'wax', and that the application of the word to an article was an indication that the material from which it was made contained no wax and was therefore pure. This is generally understood to be a reference to the ancient practice among potters and sculptors of mixing wax with their clay to make it go further or to use the wax to repair cracks and imperfections in their artefacts and thus make them appear perfect and undamaged. By extension the same adjective, when applied to a man or woman, meant that he or she was 'morally unsullied', 'pure of spirit', and thus the word became synonymous with genuineness and honesty.

Unfortunately, this explanation is complicated slightly by what may be a confusion of two Greek adjectives, either of which by happy coincidence could be used to explain the derivation of the word 'sincere'. The Latin noun *cera* is cognate with the Greek *kēros*, which also means 'wax' and has an associated adjective *akēratos*, meaning 'not coated with wax' and is therefore very close in meaning to *sincerus*. But another very similar-looking adjective, *akēratos*, from the verb *kerannumi*, 'to mix', meant 'unmixed', 'unadulterated', and this adjective could also be used metaphorically as a description of a morally untainted person.

The second possible derivation is postulated by Wyld who ignores the association with wax and states that the *-cer-* element of 'sincere' is derived from the Greek *Kēres*, Goddesses of Destruction and Decay, the Latin form of whose name, *caries*, was absorbed into English in the seventeenth century as a medical term for bone and tooth decay. Further cognates are considered to be the Sanskrit *srnati*, 'he smashes', 'he destroys', and the Anglo-Saxon for a sword, *heoru*, which is of course a weapon of destruction.

According to Homer these Kēres haunted the battlefields, draped in blood-soaked robes, together with the dreadful companions personified as Eris, 'Strife', Kudoimos, 'The Din of War', and Enuō, Goddess of Battle and companion of Ares, the God of War.

There is an obvious parallel here between the Greek and Nordic mythology, as the Kēres performed a role not dissimilar to that played by the Valkyries of Scandinavian folklore. They, too, were supposed to hover above the battlefields and, if not specifically decide who was to die, at least determine who among the dead warriors would be transported to Valhalla, the Hall of the Fallen.

There is a possible linguistic connection here also. The word Valkyrie is an Old Norse term comprising two elements: *valr*, 'the slain', and *kyrja*, 'to choose', and there may be a thematic overlap in the way the Greek *kēr* evolved in meaning. With the passage of time the Greek word acquired the significance of Fate in general as represented by the destruction and decay that awaits us all. In Homer's *Iliad*, for instance, we see how any man who is destined to die a violent death is assigned a *kēr* at birth. We also learn that Achilles' mother, Thetis, informed him that he had been assigned two *kēres* and that he had to choose which one he wanted to accept. In practical terms this meant choosing either a brief but glorious life or a long but uneventful journey to the grave.

Given the strong mythological similarities between the two cultures the linguistic connections may also be significant. If the Kēres did evolve into a concept of Destiny which involved an element of choice, then the etymological connection between it and the Old Norse verb *kyrja* may be more than coincidental.

SKETCH

A hastily drawn picture or brief verbal description, the word 'sketch' is a direct borrowing from Greek. It is derived from the word *schedios*, which had two meanings. In a spatial context it meant 'near', but in temporal expressions it meant 'all of a sudden', 'on the spur of the moment', and this second meaning gave rise to a verb *schediazō*, 'to do something without prior preparation' or 'to make an extempore speech'. The present English meaning dates from the seventeenth century.

SLOGAN

This is a direct borrowing from Irish Gaelic. The word is made up of two Irish roots, *sluagh* and *gairm*. The first element just means a large number of people and so, depending on the context, can mean 'the public', 'a crowd', 'a host', and in County Antrim can be applied to a flock of more than five hundred sheep. There is also the expression *sluagh an tighe*, which means 'the people of the house'. In the context of the derivation of the word 'slogan', however, the particular meaning of *sluagh* is 'army'.

The second element, *gairm*, means 'call', and when we put these two elements together we arrive at *gairm sluaigh*, 'a call to arms', 'proclamation of mobilization'. For some unknown reason, when the English borrowed the expression they altered the word order, corrupted it into 'sloggorne' and then it developed into its present form. The meaning we now attach to it, a catchphrase or political watchword, dates from the eighteenth century

SMASHING

Most dictionaries will tell you that this word is used in colloquial English to mean 'very good' or 'beautiful'. Some will also say that the origin is unknown, but this may not be so. It is almost certainly from the Irish Gaelic *is maith sin* (pronounced 'smaashin'), meaning 'that is good'. It is probably one of the expressions which found their way into England when there was an influx of Irish into the country in the nineteenth century.

SOAP

The immediate antecedents of this word are Germanic (for instance, the German *Seife*) and thought to be derived from the Latin *sebum*, meaning the 'fat' or 'grease' used as an aid to washing and bathing in former times. A related Latin word *oesypum* meant, more specifically, 'the fat or grease of unwashed wool', and this was a borrowing of the Greek word *oisupos*, itself derived from *oispē*, the Greek term which also meant the grease of unwashed wool. *Oispē* is derived from *ois*, 'sheep', which is cognate with Latin *ovis* and

English 'ewe'. There is a linguistic echo here in that the word 'lanolin' (Latin *lana*, 'wool', and *oleum*, 'oil') also denotes a grease obtained from sheep and used as a base for ointments and soaps.

If we trace the word 'ewe' back even further we find that it is related to the word *avi* , 'sheep' in Sanskrit, a word which originally meant a 'pet' from the adjective *avis* meaning 'devoted to' or 'attached to'. The Indo-European root from which the Greek, Sanskrit, etc., are derived is AW, 'to be pleased', 'to be satisfied'.

SOOTHSAYER

This is not a particularly common word today, but known to all who read Shakespeare. It is a compound noun made up of two elements: 'to say' and 'sooth', an old word for the 'truth'. The basic meaning of the word, therefore, is 'someone who tells the truth'.

The Anglo-Saxon *soth*, from which it is derived, is from the Indo-European root AS, 'to be', and is therefore cognate with Latin *esse*, 'to be', and basically means 'that which is'.

The connection with the verb 'to soothe' is an interesting one. We now use this verb as a synonym of 'to assuage', 'to calm' someone, but the association with Anglo-Saxo *soth* is an indication of the manner in which this calmness was achieved. The original sense was to agree with what someone was saying, to accept their version of events as being true and hence to remove all source of anger. After all, we never lose our temper with people who agree with us!

SPOON

The Anglo-Saxon word *spon* meant a 'chip' or 'shaving of wood', and this was cognate with the Greek word *sphēn*, meaning a 'wedge'. The connection is clear. The original spoons were probably no more than pieces of flat wood used for eating until somebody had the bright idea of hollowing out one end so that it could be used for scooping up liquids.

A modern German word which has retained almost the original form as the Anglo-Saxon is *der Span*, and this has retained the original meaning of 'shaving' or 'kindling'. The German for what English speakers call a spoon is *Löffel*.

The Indo-European root from which 'spoon' is derived is SPA, 'to stretch out', 'to draw out'. This same root also produced the Greek word *spathē*, which was a flattened-out stick used by weavers to periodically beat the strands of cloth so that the final product would be a tightly woven cloth. This found its way into Latin as *spatha*, then into Anglo-Saxon as *spadu*, by which time it was used with the same meaning as modern English 'spade'.

In Northern Ireland a person who is feeling a bit down in the mouth might be described as having 'a face like a Lurgan spade'. But there is no such thing as a 'Lurgan spade', nor is there any history of spade-making in Lurgan. The reason for the expression is that the English-speaking Ulstermen, hearing the Irish Gaelic *lorg an spáid*, 'the handle or shaft of the spade', confused the first two words with the town Lurgan.

SPORT

The word 'sport' now evokes images of football, cricket or tennis matches or some other similar event involving athletic confrontation, but such a connotation dates only from as recently as the sixteenth century. Prior to that the word 'disport' (of which today's word is an abbreviation) meant 'to amuse', 'to play' or just generally to enjoy oneself.

The origin of the word is the Latin *dis*, 'away', and the infinitive *portare*, 'to carry', the implication being that to 'disport oneself' was to carry oneself away from the trials and tribulations of everyday existence.

Most languages have abbreviated the word in the same way that English has, so French, German and Russian all have *sport* as the normal word to describe competitive physical activity. Spanish, however, has *el deporte*, which retains more of the original form than most.

STIGMA

In modern English the metaphorical meaning of this word has largely superseded the literal. To the Victorians divorce, illegitimacy and debt carried a 'social stigma' which really meant that anybody affected had been 'marked' or 'branded' and thus stood out from those who fitted into society's rigid concepts of conformity and convention.

The literal meaning of the Greek word *stigma* was a mark or brand which had been produced by scratching or scraping with a pointed object. The derivative verb was *stizō*, 'to prick', 'to pierce', which was derived from the Indo-European root STIG, 'to thrust', 'to smite', and the same root produced other English nouns associated with poking, piercing or stabbing such as 'stick', 'stake' and even a bee's 'sting'. It also produced the Old Norse verb *steikja*, meaning 'to roast on a stick or spit', and a piece of meat that had been thus prepared for the table was a *steik* or, in its more recognizable modern English form, a 'steak'.

Obviously, the best way to pierce skin, flesh or material is to have a stick that has been sharpened into a fine point, and the Greek verb for this activity was *kharassō*. The pointed stake or stick was then termed a *kharaks*, and this could be used for etching designs, identification marks or brands in cattle, property or anything else which needed to be singled out as having a distinguishing mark. It was even used in the design of coins and seals, and the design impressed or cut into the surface of an object in this way was known as a *kharaktēr*, an alternative term to *stigma*. This is our word 'character'.

STIRRUP

Technically speaking what we refer to as a 'stirrup' should really be termed a 'stirrup iron' as the word 'stirrup' dates from a time long before the introduction of the metal variety. The original, Anglo-Saxon form of the word was *stigrap*, a combination of two other words, *stigan*, 'to climb', and *ráp*, 'rope', so that the real meaning of 'stirrup' is 'climbing rope'.

The Anglo-Saxon *stigan* had as a derivative noun *stigel* and this developed into the word 'stile' (something to climb over). Another derivative noun from the same verb was *stigend*, 'rising', which became 'sty' (a 'rising' on the eyelid). The modern German verb *steigen*, 'to climb', is a direct descendant of the Anglo-Saxon verb and, like its forebear, is used extensively in association with travel so that varieties of the verb include: *einsteigen*, 'to get on' (a bus, train, etc.), *aussteigen*, 'to get off', and *umsteigen*, 'to change' (trains, buses, etc.). But a 'sty' on the eyelid in German is *das Gerstenkorn*. Why this should be so is not clear, as the primary meaning of *Gerstenkorn* is 'barleycorn'.

The custom of offering a departing guest a 'stirrup cup' (or 'one for the road' in modern parlance) must have been widespread as most languages have a set expression to describe that final glass of something warming. French and Spanish retain the association with 'stirrup' in their respective expressions: *coup de l'étrier* and *la del estribo*. German is less imaginative and simply calls it *ein Abschiedstrunk*, 'a farewell drink'. Irish Gaelic has *deoch an dorais*, literally the 'drink of/at the door', and Russian uses *pososhok na dorozhku*, 'a little staff or crozier for the road'.

There is, however, another interesting cognate here, the word 'saltire'. This is the heraldic term for the Cross of St Andrew and also the word which is frequently applied to the flag of Scotland. The connection between the two is that a 'saltire' cross resembles two triangular stirrups, one placed on top of the other. Linguistically the association is obvious as 'saltire' is derived from the Latin verb *salio, salire, salui, saltum*, and this in turn is related to the Greek *hallomai*, 'to leap', 'to spring'. The Latin form of the verb is evident in the Old French word for a stirrup, *saultoir*.

STRATEGY

Modern English uses this word to mean an overall plan of action intended for the successful achievement of a particular goal. It (and its related noun 'stratagem', a cunning plan) is derived from the Greek *stratēgia*, 'generalship', and *stratēgos*, 'a general'. *Stratēgos* itself is a compound noun made up of *stratos*, 'an army', 'a host', and the verb *agō*, 'to lead'. So 'strategy', strictly speaking, is the art of leading large bodies of men.

Modern English usage of the word 'general' to denote a commander of an army has its origins in the Latin adjective *generalis*, 'pertaining to the whole', 'universal'.

Modern military parlance distinguishes between 'strategic' planning, which is concerned with the overall picture of the conduct of a war, and 'tactical' planning, which is the concern of officers of lesser rank who are responsible for more localized military activity. Here, too, the origin of the word is to be found in Greek military doctrine. 'Tactics', broadly speaking, is the art of positioning one's resources in such a position as to bring about a favourable outcome in any future military contact with an enemy. The associated Greek noun and verb are *taxis*, 'position', 'arrangement', and *tassō*, 'to place'.

SUDDEN

This is another good example of how words can change meaning over time, particularly when they move from one language to another.

'Sudden' is from the Latin *subitus* (it came into English via the French, which had altered the Latin to *soudain*), which is an adjective derived from the infinitive *subire*. This in turn comprises the prefix *sub*, which basically means 'under' but also has the additional meaning of 'stealthily', 'unseen', 'underhand', and the infinitive *ire*, 'to go'. Combining the two elements, we arrive at an infinitive which means 'to approach unseen', 'to advance stealthily'. The adjective 'sudden', therefore, was really applied to occurrences that had not been anticipated rather than those characterized by speed as the word now implies.

SURGEON

Class-conscious doctors who have acquired a degree of expertise in what is probably the most demanding and prestigious field of medicine may be somewhat surprised to learn that their title means nothing more than 'manual labourer'.

The original spelling in English was 'chirurgeon', a borrowing from the French *chirurgien*, and the abstract noun denoting the activity *chirurgie*. This latter word was derived from the Greek *cheirourgia*, a compound noun made up from *cheir*, 'hand', and *ergon*, 'work', so a surgeon was originally just someone who worked with his hands. Also, the place where in former times one might expect to find a 'chirurgeon' was a 'chirurgie', the forerunner of the modern 'surgery'.

If we add the stem of *pous* (*pod-*), the Greek for 'foot', to the Greek for 'hand' we arrive at the description of somebody who specializes in hands and feet, a 'chiropodist'.

Interestingly, a translation of the Greek elements of this word into Latin produces a similar concept but in a vastly different context. The Latin for 'hand' is *manus*, and *opus* (plural *opera*) is 'work'. When these words combined and were adopted into French the form which emerged was *manoeuvre*, a word now fully integrated into English. And if we take the evolution a stage further we arrive at the word 'manure', which originally was a verb meaning 'to work the land with one's hands'. So 'to manure' a field originally meant 'to till' it, and the application of the word to the waste matter used as fertilizer was a later development.

SWASTIKA

This is associated in most people's minds with Hitler and the rise of Nazism in Germany in the 1930s. In fact the sign was an ancient symbol of good luck, and the word derives from the Sanskrit *svasti*, meaning 'well-being', 'good fortune'. The word *svasti* itself is derived from *su*, 'well', and *asti*, 'being', which is cognate with Greek *esti*, Latin *est*, French *est* and English 'is'.

Other terms for the swastika design are 'fylfot', thought to be a corruption of 'four feet', and 'gammadion', a reference to the shape being constructed from four 'gammas', the third letter of the Greek alphabet.

SYCOPHANT

This word seems to have altered its meaning considerably over time. The *sukophantai* in Ancient Greece were quasi-professional litigants who made a living out of bringing people to court, sometimes on very flimsy evidence, and then making a killing when a guilty verdict was brought in. It also appears that it was not unknown for citizens of Athens to be blackmailed by these *sukophantai* and threatened with legal proceedings for relatively minor misdeeds if they did not pay up. In fact, the legal system was such that it left itself open to all kinds of abuse, and these informers could and did use their skills to ingratiate themselves with the rich and powerful.

The word itself is almost certainly a compound noun comprising *sukon*, 'fig', and *phainō*, 'to show'. It has been suggested that the original *sukophantai* were so called because they spied on and then denounced people who were trading illegally in figs by exporting them from Attica. On the other hand, the word may simply have been coined as a colourful description of those who displayed a feigned sweetness in order to gain favour and win the confidence of those in positions of authority.

TALK

This is thought to be the only word in English borrowed directly from Lithuanian, which has *tulkas* for 'talk' and *tulkoti* for 'interpreter'. It is further believed that the word is cognate with the Russian *tolk*, meaning 'sense', and the verb *tolkovat'*, 'to interpret', 'to explain', and the first syllable of the German word *Dolmetscher*, 'an interpreter'.

TANTALIZE

This verb has its origin in the noun 'tantalus', a drink stand in which the bottles are visible but locked away. It was so named after

Tantalus who, in Greek mythology, was the son of Jupiter and father of Niobe and Pelops. The story goes that he divulged heavenly secrets to mere mortals and was condemned to spend eternity in the underworld close to food and drink that moved away from him as he attempted to satisfy his everlasting hunger and thirst.

TARIFF

Strictly speaking a 'tariff' is an official list indicating the taxes imposed by a government on imports and exports, but the word is frequently used to mean a table of prices and charges. The word is a direct borrowing from the Arabic *ta'rif,* meaning 'notification', from another Arabic word *'arf,* 'knowledge'.

TATTOO

When we hear this word we probably think first of all of those naked ladies and entwined snakes and dragons so beloved of people who like to adorn their bodies with images etched into their skin. In this context the word 'tattoo' is the Tahitian word for such drawings and is thought to have been brought back to England from Polynesia (Greek for 'many islands') by the eighteenth-century seafarers who sailed to that part of the world.

The other kind of tattoo, the display of military skills, bears no linguistic relationship to the skin drawing whatever. In this sense 'tattoo' is a corruption of the Dutch word *taptoe,* meaning either 'the tap (-room) is closed' or 'the tap on the barrel has been turned off'. In seventeenth-century Holland the closing of drinking houses, taprooms, etc., was accompanied by a drum beat or bugle call which was a signal for the soldiers to return to barracks for the night. The combination of bugle and drum, sounded at night, formed the basis of what we now understand by the term 'military tattoo'.

TAVERN

The Latin word *taberna* designated any kind of hut, shop or booth and is thought to be a distorted form of an earlier word *traberna* which was derived from the word *trabs,* the basic meaning of which was 'beam' or 'timber', and thus provides an example of how the building material can, by extension, come to refer as well to the finished construction.

The Roman term for a small-scale *taberna* was a *tabernaculum* which described the type of dwelling which we would call a tent. This word was borrowed by the Israelites to mean a temporary shelter, and then it came to designate, more specifically, a transportable temple which could accompany them as they moved from place to place. Later still it came to be applied to the receptacle for the Host in churches and is, of course, the origin of the word adopted into English as 'tabernacle'.

TAWDRY

Now an adjective used to describe anything considered 'cheap and cheerful', gaudy or showy. But the word is actually a contraction of 'St Awdrey's lace', a general term applied to the inexpensive laces, baubles and trinkets sold at the medieval fairs held on St Awdrey's Day, 17 October, on the Isle of Ely in Cambridgeshire.

Awdrey (archaic spelling of Audrey) was the daughter of Anna, Queen of East Anglia in the seventh century AD. As a child she is reputed to have had an inordinate fondness for sparkling necklaces, and in later life, when she developed what is thought to have been throat cancer, she blamed it on her earlier preoccupation with flashy adornment.

And 'gaudy'? This word is derived from a now no longer found noun, 'gaud', meaning 'show' or 'ornament'. The word passed into English from Latin *gaudium*, 'gladness', 'celebration', which is cognate with the Greek verbs *gaiō* and *gētheō*, 'to rejoice'. The same source gave us the words 'joy', 'to enjoy' (originally to celebrate by adorning oneself) and 'jewel'. The close association between celebration and adornment can be seen in the Spanish cognate noun *joya*, which does not mean 'joy' but 'jewellery'.

TAXI

This word now refers to a mode of conveyance but is really an abbreviated form of the French word *taximètre* which was a device for measuring the distance travelled and calculating the fare due. The French word itself is a hybrid made up from the Greek *metreō*, 'to measure', and the Latin *taxare*, the frequentative infinitive of *tango, tangere, tetigi, tactum*, meaning basically 'to touch' but also 'to handle' and, by extension, 'to weigh' and thus 'to estimate'.

TENTERHOOKS

If we describe someone as 'being on tenterhooks' we imply that he or she is in a state of anxiety and feeling extremely nervous.

A 'tenterhook' was originally a special type of hook designed to keep hanging tapestries tightly stretched over a frame or 'tenter' when wet so that they would dry straight. The Middle English for such a tapestry was *tentoure*, borrowed from French *tenture*, and this in turn was derived from the Latin verb *tendo, tendere, tetendi, tensum* (or *tentum*), 'to stretch'. The same Latin verb produced another Medieval Latin word, *tenta*, and this eventually became the modern English 'tent'. It also gave the modern Spanish for a shop, *tienda*. The connection is obvious: the original shops would probably have been no more than a piece of canvas, or some such material, stretched over a few poles to provide some protection from the elements, just as our 'tent' is supposed to shield campers from the elements.

The Latin infinitive *tendere* was derived from the Greek *teinō*, which meant 'to stretch' and 'to draw' (a bow), and the noun associated with it, *tonos*, could be either a rope or sinew (that is, something which is stretched) or a musical note or tone. It also gave us the concept of 'toning up' muscles, etc.

Other words and expressions common in modern English which can be traced back to the verb *teinō* include 'tense' (under strain), to tend towards (to be pulled in a certain direction) and even the adjective 'thin', as anything which is stretched will always become thinner.

A compound of the Greek *teinō* was *anateinō*, meaning 'to stretch out', 'to elongate', 'to spread out', and this gave us the word 'antenna'.

THEATRE

The theatre is arguably one of the most important cultural legacies bequeathed by Ancient Greece to the modern world. Tragedians such as Euripedes and Sophocles can be said to have laid the foundations of virtually all that we now consider dramatic art. So it should come as no surprise that almost all European languages have adopted the Greek word (albeit in modified form) to define the activity.

'Theatre' is from the Greek noun *theatron*, which literally meant 'a place for seeing', derived as it was from the verb *theaomai*, 'to behold', 'to gaze at'. If a *theatron* was constructed as a circle so that the action on stage could be seen 'in the round', it was called an *amphitheatron* (the prefix *amphi-* meaning 'around', 'on all sides'), which gave us the word 'amphitheatre'.

Events performed on stage can be referred to collectively as 'drama' and for the origin of this word too we need look no further than Greek. The root verb is *draō*, which simply means 'to do'. In other words, 'drama' means nothing more than 'those things which are done' on stage. And if the actors and all those who work in a theatre do so in a manner which can be described as 'effective', the equivalent adjective a twenty-first-century Greek would use to describe such activity is *drastikos*, also from *draō*, and this is the original meaning of the modern English word 'drastic'.

If we take things a little further and consider the different types of on-stage performance, modern audiences usually choose between going to see a comedy or a tragedy. And yet again the terminology is Greek.

A 'tragedy', as we now understand the word, is likely to deal with serious topics in a thought-provoking manner and to produce emotional responses such as sadness and tears. It may come as a surprise, therefore, to learn that the word 'tragedy' is derived from the Greek *tragos*, meaning 'a goat'. It is difficult to give a definitive

173

explanation as to why this should be so, as a number of theories have been opined. One explanation, for instance, is that among the Ancient Greeks it was simply the custom for actors in 'tragedies' to wear goat-skins to distinguish them from the more light-hearted actors who took part in comedies. Another theory is that the serious drama was performed at festivals devoted to Dionysos, God of the Vine, and that he was regularly represented as being half man and half goat. But as comedies were also performed at such festivals this seems an unlikely explanation. Yet another theory, and the one which seems to offer the most likely explanation, is that the Dorians invented the *tragōdia* (literally a 'goat-song') originally to accompany the solemn rites associated with the sacrifice of a goat. These songs, with the passage of time, came to be used as the accompaniment to theatrical performances, and then later still the musical content was dispensed with but the gravitas and solemnity which we now associate with serious productions was retained.

'Comedy' is also the subject of some discussion and difference of opinion among etymologists. Some adhere to the belief that the word is derived from the Greek *kōmos*, meaning 'revelry' or 'merry-making', and others maintain that it is from another noun, *kōmē*, 'village', and that the antecedent of 'comedy' was *kōmēdia*, 'mirthful spectacle'.

The most interesting theory, however, is that posited by Skeat, who suggests that the first element, *kōmos*, was specifically a revelry at which the guests lay down as they ate, drank and watched the entertainment. He therefore maintains that the root of the word is *koimaō*, 'to lull to rest' or 'to put to sleep'. The same verb also gave us the word 'cemetery', so, if Skeat is correct in his supposition 'comedy' and 'cemetery' are virtually the same word.

THERAPY

We now use this verb to mean exclusively medical treatment, but originally the Greek verb from which it is derived, *therapeuō*, meant 'to worship or pay honour to the gods', although it was also used in many other expressions and with many other meanings. It meant 'to flatter', 'to pay court to', 'to cultivate the land', and appeared in expressions such as *therapeuō to paron*, 'to provide for the present', and *therapeuō hemeran*, 'to observe a holy day'. Gradually the word came to take on a narrower range of meanings, and by Homer's time it had acquired a general meaning of paying attention to or being in attendance on someone. The noun *therapōn* is used by Homer to mean a companion at arms, possibly as a squire to a knight in the Middle Ages, or just a companion (although of inferior rank) such as Patroclus was to Achilles. The important thing to note is that *therapontes* were servants who rendered their services of their own accord and were not *douloi*, slaves. That is, except on the island of Chios, where the word did imply slavery.

Our word 'therapy', the application of medical treatment, has only enjoyed this meaning since the nineteenth century.

THRESHOLD

The first part of this word, etymologists agree, is the verb 'to thresh', which is simply an older form of 'to thrash'. This verb is used exclusively in modern English to mean 'to beat', either literally or figuratively, but the original sense of the word referred to the crashing noise which accompanied such an action. Skeat suggests that it was probably first used to describe the noise of thunder but then came to be applied to the cracking sound made by a flail when corn is being threshed. Its application to sound as opposed to an activity is reflected in the fact that the word is cognate with the Russian verb *treskat*, 'to snap', 'to crackle', 'to pop'.

The second part of the word is the subject of some disagreement and discussion. Ayto and Onions maintain that it has not been explained etymologically, but Wyld and Skeat opine that the element '-old' is derived from the Middle English *wold*, which in turn is derived from the Anglo-Saxon *wald*, meaning 'wood' or 'forest'. This same root reappears in the modern German *Wald*, which is the modern English 'weald' as in 'the Weald of Kent', just as its older counterpart *wold* appears in place-names such as Southwold and the Cotswolds.

175

Skeat suggests that the word 'threshold', then, was originally 'thresh-wold', that is, a piece of timber placed underneath a door which was 'thrashed' or beaten as people came and went. This sounds slightly implausible, and another possibility is that the reference was originally to a piece of timber strategically positioned to prevent the newly threshed wheat from escaping beneath the door.

THROMBOSIS

The associations with serious and potentially life-threatening medical conditions which this word evokes for most of us make the origin of the word somewhat surprising. The Greek verb at its root is *trephō*, which basically meant 'to nourish', 'to rear', but had a secondary meaning of 'to make firm or solid'. Such a verb should conjure up images of healthy, well-fed children and sturdy adult members of a society that appreciates the value of sensible nutrition.

However, the verb's secondary meaning produced two further nouns, *trophalis*, meaning 'curdled milk' or 'cheese', and *thrombos*, which could be applied to almost any lump or piece which had broken off a larger whole. The Greeks' medical knowledge was such that they too understood the dangers of thickening blood and so used the word *thrombos* with precisely the meaning we attach to it today, a blood-clot.

The word *thrombōsis*, to the Greeks, meant 'the process of becoming curdled'.

TIME

The proverb 'time and tide wait for no man' is tautological. 'Time' and 'tide' are really the same word, the latter surviving now to describe the ebb and flow of the sea and in compounds such as the church festivals 'Eastertide', 'Yuletide' and archaisms such as 'noontide' and 'eventide'. The reason for the confusion is probably due to the fact that Anglo-Saxon had *tima* for time in general and *tid* which also meant time in general but more specifically 'an hour'. The latter form of the word is cognate with modern Danish *tid* and German *Zeit*.

The Anglo-Saxon noun *tid* produced a verb *tidan*, 'to happen', that is, to take place at a particular point in time. Reports of such events were 'tidings' as in the phrases 'glad tidings' and 'tidings of great joy'.

Another somewhat archaic but etymologically related phrase occasionally used in modern English is 'woe betide'. If we say 'woe betide anyone who . . .', what we are really saying is 'may grief happen to anyone who . . .'

Modern English uses the word 'tidy' to mean 'neat', 'everything in its proper place'. This, however, is a slight shift of meaning as this usage has come into English directly from the German, with *zeitig* as an adjective meaning 'timely', 'occurring at the correct time'. Obviously, the concept of accuracy and appropriateness has not changed but English has moved from a temporal to a spatial meaning.

TOILET

It is now considered somewhat old-fashioned to use this word in reference to anything other than the most basic of bodily functions. Formerly, however, the word was virtually synonymous with dressing, and the phrase 'at one's toilet' meant nothing more than getting dressed; and 'ladies' toilets' used to be just an alternative for ladies' gowns or dresses.

The association with dressing betrays the French origins of the word. *Toilette* in French is the diminutive of *toile*, meaning 'cloth', and one suggestion is that the phrase 'at one's toilet' arose from the custom among ladies of draping their shoulders with a cloth when they were having their hair groomed. In time the expression acquired the expanded meaning of getting dressed in general.

The French word *toile* was adapted from the Latin *tela*, which meant anything that had been woven and was derived from the verb *texo, texere, texui, textum*, 'to weave', and as such is cognate with 'texture' and even with the word 'text', the original meaning of which was something that had been woven. In a further development of the word, a material which had been woven in such a manner as to produce a particularly fine cloth was described in

Latin as being *subtilis* (thought to be from an earlier form *subtexlis*) or 'finely woven', and this has given us the adjective 'subtle'.

As the Latin *tela* was associated with the verb 'to weave' it also meant a web, and this survives today in the Spanish *telaraña*, 'a spider's web' (*tela* plus *araña*, 'spider').

Most European languages have adopted the word 'toilet' and use it to mean exactly what it means in English. Some, however, do have native words which survive alongside the Anglo-French import. Spanish, for instance, has *los servicios* (literally 'the services') and *los aseos* (from the verb *asearse*, 'to smarten /tidy oneself up'). German has *die Toilette* but also the older *das Abort*, which literally means 'the away place', 'the place set to one side'. Russian generally uses *tualet* now but also has *ubornaya*, short for *ubornaya komnata*, 'the room for tidying oneself up', from the verb *ubrat'*, 'to tidy', 'to clean up'. In colloquial speech Russian also has *nuzhnik*, literally 'the necessary', and the humorous euphemism for 'to go to the toilet', *idti tuda, kuda tsar' idyot peshkom*, 'to go where the tsar goes on foot'.

Travellers to Eastern Europe have to be careful not to confuse their Slavonic languages, as there are a great many so-called 'false friends'. One such is the Czech word *zachod*, which means 'toilet', but the same word in Russian means either 'sunset' or 'brief visit'. The link is probably the idea of popping in somewhere on the way to somewhere else.

TOY

It is possible (but some etymologists disagree) that the origin of this word is the Greek *teukhos*, meaning 'tool' or 'implement' (from *teukhō*, 'to construct', 'to create', 'to forge', etc.). With the passage of time this word went on to develop a further meaning of 'book' and as such is one of the elements in the word *pentateukhos*, 'Pentateuch', the first five books of the Old Testament.

The word 'toy' acquired the meaning of a 'plaything' in English, but in languages such as Dutch and German its cognate has retained the meaning of an 'instrument', hence the former has *tuig*, 'utensil', and the latter *Zeug*, also an 'implement', frequently found in compounds such as *Spielzeug*, 'plaything', 'toy', and *Feuerzeug*, 'cigarette lighter'.

TRAVEL

Travel in the twenty-first century is relatively easy. Within a matter of a few hours we can be at destinations which our forebears had probably never even heard of, let alone visited. We can drive to an airport, get on a plane and be halfway across the world in less than a day. The same journey, a mere century ago, would have taken weeks if not months.

For our ancestors travel was not just a lengthy process, it was also a very difficult one. It involved a lot of hard work, and this is reflected in the etymology of the word itself. 'Travel' is virtually the same word as the French and Spanish words *travailler* and *trabajar*, both of which simply mean 'to work', and are cognate with the older English 'travail'.

The Medieval Latin word from which these are all derived was *trepalium* (itself a contraction of *tria*, 'three', and *palus*, 'a rod'), which was a three-pronged instrument of torture used, presumably, to encourage people to work harder.

TREACLE

This is not a word used very much in everyday speech but nevertheless holds some surprises for the professional or amateur etymologist. We now think of it as a thick, black substance obtained from the sugar cane, but the word originally applied to any medicinal compound, especially those which were thought to be antidotes to poison. The word has come down to us via the French *triacle* and Latin *theriaca* from the Greek *thēriaka pharmaka*, meaning 'animal compounds', as the substance was produced by Greek doctors as medicine used in cases of patients being bitten by wild and/or venomous creatures.

The *thēr* of *thēriaca* is the Greek for 'wild animal', and it shows up again in the German *das Tier* and our word 'deer'. The same root also accounts for the 'der' in our word 'wilderness' which was originally a place where wild animals roamed (Anglo-Saxon *wild deor* = wild animal). *Deer* and *deor* can be traced even further back to the hypothetical Indo-European noun *dheusom*, 'a breathing animal', and as such is cognate with the Russian *dusha*, meaning 'soul'.

But perhaps even more surprising is the connection with the verb 'bewilder'. If someone is startled or shocked we say that they are bewildered, meaning literally that they are so perplexed that they have lost their bearings and feel as if they have been transported into the middle of a wilderness.

TREE

In Ancient Greek the word *drus* meant specifically 'an oak' whereas the blanket word for 'tree' was *dendron*. *Drus* eventually changed into English 'tree' and is still recognizable in the word 'dryad' meaning a wood-nymph. *Dendron* also made its way into English but in more specialized contexts and compound nouns such as 'rhododendron' (Greek *rhodon dendron*, 'rose tree'), 'dendrology' (the scientific study of trees) and 'dendrochronology' (the dating of timber by studying its annual growth rings).

The Greek *drus* turned up in various forms in many of the world's languages. In Welsh it became *derwen*, still meaning an oak, and the origin of the word *derwydd*, 'druid'. But in Russian the word changed into *derevo*, the general word for any tree.

In the case of Russian there is a fascinating twist. A close relative of the word in its Russian form is *zdorov'e*, 'health', a connection brought about perhaps by the image of health and strength created by tall, majestic trees.

There is a distinct parallel here with what happened when the word entered English by way of Latin. *Drus* reappeared in Latin as *durus*, 'hard', and this of course is the origin of English 'durable'. But another word directly related to it is the Anglo-Saxon *trum*, 'strong', 'healthy', which in modern English is 'trim' in both its verbal and adjectival usage. If we describe somebody as 'looking very trim' we imply that he or she looks fit and well, and if we trim a bush or tree we get rid of the dead wood so that the plant can grow strong and healthy.

This linguistic association between trees and health is echoed in the Latin *robur* (which had an earlier form *robus*), meaning 'oak', and its derivative adjective *robustus*, 'hard', 'firm', 'made of oak', which is the origin of our word 'robust'.

TRIUMPH

In modern English this word is virtually synonymous with 'victory'. The explanation for this is that the word's immediate antecedent is the Latin *triumphus,* a victory procession for which permission might be granted by the Roman Senate to a general returning from a successful military campaign.

The Romans inherited the word from the Greek *thriambos*, which was both a hymn to Bacchus, the god of wine and revelry, and an alternative name for the god himself. So the original concept was merriment and rejoicing, for whatever reason, and the transfer of meaning to the military activity which gave rise to such excitement was a later development.

TRIVIAL

There are three explanations of the origin of this word. The first traces the derivation back to ancient Rome and the Latin words *tri*, 'three', and *via*, 'road', which combined to give the noun *trivium*. This literally meant a place where three roads met, but it came to be used to designate any open street or public place. The adjective derived from it, *trivialis*, had a literal meaning of 'pertaining to public places' but also acquired a metaphorical meaning of 'ordinary' or 'commonplace', so to describe an article as *trivialis* was really akin to saying that it could be picked up on any street corner.

The second explanation is derived from medieval concepts of the definition of a 'good' education. The higher course of study at medieval universities was known as the *quadrivium*, that is to say, a study of the four disciplines: geometry, music, arithmetic and astronomy. The lesser, more basic subjects of study were grammar, rhetoric and logic, and these three were known collectively as the *trivium*. In other words, to medieval scholars some subjects of academic study were considered 'trivial' in comparison with others.

The third explanation (but the one which probably carries least weight) is that the word 'trivial' is not derived from the Latin for 'three' but is in fact a combination of the Greek verb *tribō*, 'to rub', and the Latin noun *via* and that a *trivium* is a 'well-trodden road'.

TROGLODYTE

A cave-dweller; the literal meaning of the word is 'one who creeps into holes'. The word is comprised of two Greek roots: *trōglē*, 'a hole', from the verb *trōgō*, 'to gnaw', 'to bite a hole in', and *dutēs*, literally 'a diver' from the verb *duō*, 'to plunge into', 'to make one's way into'.

The same Greek verb *trōgō* also produced the noun *trōktēs*, 'nibbler', which generated the Latin word *tructa*, and this became the English term for the freshwater fish, the trout.

TROPHY

The original trophies were artefacts of war which were hung on a tree to show that the enemy had been routed and then brought home as a symbol of triumph. The word entered English from the French *trophée*, an adapted form of the Latin *tropaeum*, and both were derived from the Greek noun *tropaion*. The word *tropaion* itself came from another noun, *tropē*, 'a turn', and the verb *trepō*, 'to turn'. In other words, a trophy was originally a sword, helmet, etc., dropped by the enemy and brought home by the victor as proof that the enemy had 'turned' and fled.

TRY

Modern English uses this verb with several apparently different meanings. It can be used as a synonym for 'attempt'; it can apply to the legal process of causing somebody to defend him or herself in court; and it can be used with the meaning of 'to test'. Interestingly, all three meanings stem from the same source, which appears to have little association with the modern word.

The Greek verb from which 'to try' is derived is *tribō*. Basically, this verb meant 'to rub' but with special reference to rubbing corn between the fingers in order to separate the grain from the husk. The process involved a certain degree of selection, and eventually the verb acquired the more generalized, metaphorical meaning of sorting out what was good from what was bad, and this produced the Middle English verb *trien*, 'to select', and the Old French *trier*, 'to sift'. It is easy to see how this led to the modern usage. If we 'try on' a new coat, for example, we are deciding whether or not to single it out from the others as the one we want to buy. If a criminal is brought to trial, the implication is that those who sit in judgement will weigh up the evidence and attempt to separate the truth from the lies.

When the basic Greek verb was used with the prefix *dia-* the resultant verb had several meanings. *Diatribō* emphasized that the action occupied a longer time that the basic verb. Eventually the time element acquired greater importance that the action, and so *diatribō* came to mean 'to spend time doing something'. This then gave rise to the noun *diatribē*, meaning 'pastime'. As one of the pastimes of the Ancient Greeks was conversation and discourse the noun acquired yet another meaning, 'discussion' or 'argument'. In the nineteenth century the word passed into English as 'diatribe', but by this time it was limited in meaning to criticism delivered in an aggressive manner.

Other words cognate with the original Greek verb *tribō* include 'attrition', a gradual wearing down; 'detriment', originally damage caused by rubbing; and 'detritus', now used synonymously with waste matter but originally debris left after erosion. Finally, we should also mention the adjective 'trite'. Now defined in the dictionary as 'lacking novelty or freshness', it is perhaps better thought of as 'well worn' as in an oft-repeated argument or hackneyed phrase or expression.

Another cognate noun is 'tribulation', that which wears us down.

So when we talk about 'trials and tribulations' we are to a certain extent repeating ourselves.

u

UMBRELLA

There are two words in English which are used to denote supposedly different but in fact identical means of protection from the elements. Although virtually identical in form, an umbrella is designed to protect us from the rain and a parasol is designed to protect us from the sun. Linguistically, however, they both refer to protection from the sun as 'parasol' is an Italian compound word made up of *para-* (a prefix derived from the verb *parare*, 'to ward off') and *sol*, 'sun', and so simply means something along the lines of 'designed to ward off the sun'. 'Umbrella' has a very similar meaning as it came into English via the Latin word *umbraculum* (from the noun *umbra*, 'shadow', 'shade'), which designated either a place shielded from the harsh rays of the sun or a parasol.

Other European languages give a better idea of the use for which umbrellas are designed. French has *parapluie*, which is *para-* again combined with *pluie*, 'rain'; Spanish has *paraguas*, which is very similar to the French but is for warding off 'the waters'. German is perhaps the most accurate as it has *Regenschirm*, literally 'rain protection'.

USHER

We now think of an usher as someone who shows us to our seat in a theatre or in church, but originally he would have been a kind of doorman who doubled up as a porter. We have received the word from the Old French *ussier* (or *huissier*), and this was derived from the Latin *ostiarius*, the man whose job it was to stand at the door (*ostium*) to receive guests (and, presumably, keep out the unbidden ones!).

Ostium was derived from the word *os*, 'mouth', which has also given us the adjective 'oral'. The diminutive form of *os* was *osculum*, which not only meant 'little mouth' but also a 'kiss', which is the basis of the word used in mathematics when two curves or surfaces come into contact and are said to be 'osculating'.

V

VACCINATE

We now have our children vaccinated again against measles, whooping cough and a whole range of other nasty illnesses, but the original 'vaccination' was performed by Edward Jenner in 1796 when he injected a child with the cowpox virus as a means of protecting the child against smallpox. The association with cows provided the new word, thought to have been first used in its French form *vacciner* in about 1803, derived as it was from the Latin *vacca*, 'cow'. *Vacca* is cognate with the Sanskrit *vacati*, 'it cries', 'it lows', which is also etymologically linked to the Latin *vox* , from which are derived the words 'vocal' and 'voice'.

An alternative to 'vaccinate' is the verb 'inoculate', which is directly connected linguistically with the English word 'eye', however forced the etymology may appear. 'Eye' is from the Indo-European root AK, 'to see', and is cognate with now archaic Russian *oko*, the Greek dialect form *okkos*, Anglo-Saxon *eáge*, German *Auge* and Sanskrit *aksha*. Another cognate noun which can be added to this list is the Latin *oculus*, which also meant 'eye' but had an additional meaning of the 'bud' of a plant. This gave rise to the infinitive *inoculare*, which meant 'to graft on to', 'to engraft', 'to implant', hence the connection with 'inoculations': protection from disease by the deliberate implanting of a virus into a body. This meaning dates from the seventeenth century.

VETERINARY (SURGEON)

When we take our cats, dogs or budgies to see 'the vet' we probably never think of why a doctor who specializes in sick animals is called a 'vet'. Few of us stop to consider, for instance, that the word dates from prehistoric times and that it has linguistic threads which spread out over many countries and many civilizations.

The word 'veterinary' in its present form has come down to us from the Latin word *veterinus*, an adjective meaning 'belonging to beasts of burden' from the noun *veterinae*, 'beasts of burden'. *Veterinae* was from the adjective *vetus*, 'old'. The implication here is that in the ancient world animals which were too old for any more useful tasks were used as beasts of burden. The original 'vets' must have been employed solely for the purpose of tending to their needs and comfort.

The Romans got their word *vetus* from the Greek *etos*, 'year'. In primitive Greek times (*c.* 500 BC) *etos* had been pronounced *wetos* (the 'w' sound had been written with a digamma, a letter which was discarded about 500 BC when the 'w' sound disappeared from Greek).

Other cognate words are 'veteran' in English, *vieux* in French and *viejo* in Spanish, the last two meaning 'old'. The Russian word *vetkhij* also means old or ancient (as in *Vetkhij Zavet*, the Old Testament) but more usually conveys the impression of dilapidation and ruin.

A further Latin derivative of *vetus* was *veteranus*, which also meant 'old' but was used particularly in the phrase *milites veterani*, 'old soldiers', the expression from which we derive our word 'veteran'.

VIOLIN

Skeat's explanation is that 'violin' and 'fiddle' have both come down to us via the Italian *viola* from the Latin word *vitula*, meaning 'calf' or 'heifer'. Presumably the connection is that these instruments were played at festivals where the custom was 'to be joyful', 'to skip like a calf', the Latin infinitive for which is either *vitulor* or *vitulare*. This association also explains the linguistic association with the word 'veal'.

VIRUS

The Latin noun *virus* meant both 'slimy liquid' and 'snake's venom' and was linguistically related to the Greek noun *iós*, which in its earlier form of *wisos* is recognizably cognate with the Sanskrit *visam*, 'poison', and *vesati*, 'it melts', 'it liquefies'. So already in primitive times the observational association had been made between certain slimy liquids and illness, even though viruses as we now know them remained a discovery for the distant future.

Virus is also cognate with another Latin word, *viscum*, which meant both 'birdlime' (a sticky substance made from mistletoe berries and painted on trees to trap birds) and 'mistletoe', and this has given us our words 'viscous', 'viscosity', etc. The Greek cousin of *viscus* was *iksos* (thought to be from an earlier *wiksos*), and both the Latin and Greek words are cognate with the modern Russian *vishnya*, 'cherry'.

The word 'mistletoe' itself is one over which there is less than total agreement among etymologists. All seem to agree that the second element of the word, 'toe', is from the Anglo-Saxon *tan*, meaning 'twig', but the origin of the first part, 'mistle', is disputed. Ayto and Onions claim that the derivation of this part of the word cannot be explained, whereas Skeat and Wyld agree that it can be traced back to the Indo-European root MIGH or MIG, 'to sprinkle', and that its present form is derived from the Old Dutch *mist*, meaning 'birdlime', and modern German *Mist*, 'dung', 'manure'. Skeat and Wyld also point out that other cognates here include the Greek *omikhlē*, 'fog', 'misty air' (hence the English 'mist'), and the Russian *mgla*, meaning 'gloom'. At least there seems to be little doubt here that concepts of dampness and gloom coalesced linguistically at one time.

The Greek noun *omikhlē* is related to the verb *omikhō*, which appeared in Latin as *mingo, mingere, minxi, mictum*, 'to pass water', and gave us our word 'micturition'. Skeat also states that original meaning of *mist* was 'urine', so that the fact that it is now the German for 'dung' shows a certain shift of meaning.

It would appear, therefore, that linguistically speaking there is a common denominator here involving dampness, stickiness, unpleasantness and disease which has followed divergent paths over the course of time.

WACK

'Wack' (and its variant 'wacker') is a common form of address used among Liverpudlians. If you look the word up in a dictionary the chances are that you will merely be informed that the origin is unknown. However, it is almost certain that the word entered English during the eighteenth and nineteenth centuries when there was a large influx of Irish immigrants to England via Liverpool. Many of these immigrants would have been Gaelic speaking, and in Gaelic the word for 'son' is *mac* (as in MacTaggart, son of a priest, and MacTavish, son of Thomas, etc.). Now in Gaelic certain changes take place at the beginnings of words under certain linguistic conditions. For instance, if we wish to change 'son' to 'my son' in Irish we have to change *mac* to *mo mhac*. But this is then pronounced 'mo wack'. There is just one problem about this theory, and that is that when addressing someone in Irish the vocative case has to be used and the vocative of *mo mhac* is *a mhic* (pronounced 'a vic'). But then again, when the Scousers borrowed the term, they were probably not too concerned with the intricacies of Gaelic grammar!

In Irish Gaelic the word *mac* is not restricted to 'son'. It can also mean 'warrior' or 'follower' and is used in a way which seems unusual to non-Gaelic speakers to form compound nouns and in set expressions. Consider, for example, the following:

> *mac doirche*, literally 'son of darkness', means 'illegitimate son'
> *mac leighinn*, literally 'son of learning', means 'student' and
>   has become the surname MacLean
> *mac tíre*, literally 'son of the land', means 'wolf'
> *mac an óil*, literally 'son of drink', means 'an innkeeper'

mac seo, literally 'son of a show', means 'a trickster'
mac alla, literally 'son of the cliff', means 'an echo'
mac ghall, literally 'son of a foreigner', is an alternative term for 'an Englishman'.

But the most interesting example is *mac beathadh*, literally 'the son of life', which is an Irish description for 'a sinless man' and has evolved into the surname Macbeth. So the interesting question is: Do we know if Shakespeare was aware of the irony when he wrote 'the Scottish play' with the central character as the embodiment of man's capacity for evil?

The other term for a native of Liverpool is, of course, a 'scouser'. This is believed to be an abbreviated form of 'lobscouse', a culinary delicacy consisting of meat, veg and ship's biscuit which was introduced to the port by the Dutch and Scandinavian sailors who tarried there in its heyday. Modern Danish and Norwegian still have *labskovs* and *lapskaus* respectively for 'stew', and both words are associated with the German word *labbrig*, meaning 'sloppy' or 'mushy' when applied to food.

WAR

Cognate with the French *guerre*, Spanish *guerra*, etc., the English word is most closely allied to Old High German *werren*, 'to bring confusion', and modern German *verwirren*, 'to confuse', 'to perplex'. It is also seen in modern German expressions such as *er ist wirr im Kopf*, 'he's confused in the head', and *alles lag wirr durcheinander*, 'everything was in chaos'.

It is also cognate with the Greek verb *errō*, which had originally been written with a digamma and was thus pronounced *werrō*, and basically meant 'to walk with difficulty', 'to limp', but it also had a secondary meaning of 'to come to ruin', 'to perish', and this is the basis of its association with war.

'Warfare' is a compound noun in which the '-fare' element is again German, *fahren*, 'to travel', so that the word really means 'to travel about causing confusion'.

189

The Indo-European root of this word is WAR, 'to twist', 'to turn', which means that other words cognate with 'war' are 'furrow' and 'furlong' (originally the distances ploughed before turning round). It is also cognate with the word 'worse'. In modern English this is used as the comparative adjective and adverb of 'bad', but its original meaning was 'more complicated or confused'.

WASSAIL

The ancient custom of 'wassailing' practised at Christmas has surprising linguistic connections. The origin of the word is the Anglo-Saxon *wes hál*, where *wes* is the singular imperative of the verb *wesan*, 'to be', and *hál* is the same word as modern English 'whole'. So 'wassailing' is wishing somebody good health by telling them to 'be whole'.

Hál is also the modern English word 'hale' in expressions such as 'hale and hearty' and 'hello', and can be traced back to the Greek *kalos*, meaning 'beautiful', which illustrates that the concept of a link between health and beauty is not such a modern one.

Another connection, however, is between *hál* and the German *heil*, which also means 'whole' but is also used for 'long live' in expressions such as *heil dem König!*, 'long live the King', and the Nazi exhortation *Heil Hitler!*

WEAPON

A weapon is any object used to inflict harm, injury or damage on an opponent or enemy. The origin of the word seems to have been lost in the mists of time, but we do know that it is of Germanic provenance and is connected with the Anglo-Saxon *waepen*, Middle English *wepen*, Icelandic *vopn* and modern German *die Waffe*. The modern German word also has an expanded meaning of a military unit in expressions such as *die Luftwaffe* (air force) and the Waffen SS or Waffenschutzstaffel, Hitler's infamous 'armed protection unit'.

A word which is not obviously connected with weaponry, but nevertheless is, is 'panoply'. We now use this word to mean 'a complete set' or 'a splendid array'. Its original Greek meaning, however, was 'a full set of equipment' with which to go to war, and to the Ancient Greeks this meant a shield, helmet, breastplate, greaves (leg protectors), a sword and a spear. Such a warrior was known as a *hoplitēs* or hoplite. The Greek word *panoplia* was a compound noun made up of *hoplon*, which originally meant any implement but came to mean 'implement of war', and the prefix *pan*, 'all', so that *panoplia* meant 'all the armour'. The noun *hoplon* was derived from verb *hoplizō*, which meant 'to prepare', 'to train', and was used generally to mean to equip somebody with whatever tools were needed to allow them to complete the task. This eventually acquired the meaning of 'to provide soldiers with the armour and weapons necessary for waging war'.

WEIRD

When Shakespeare described the witches in Macbeth as the 'weird sisters' he did not intend the adjective to convey the meaning it conveys today. The word now is synonymous with 'strange', 'mysterious' and 'inexplicable', but it only acquired this meaning in the nineteenth century. Prior to that it meant 'controlling the destinies of men', and this was the implication behind Shakespeare's use of the word.

Earlier still, however, 'weird' was not an adjective but a noun meaning the same as fate or destiny and was derived from the Anglo-Saxon for fate, *wyrd*, which was in turn from the verb *weorthen* (modern German *werden*), meaning 'to become'. The literal meaning of the original noun was therefore 'that which will be'. By Shakespeare's time the meaning had evolved so that people described as 'weird' had the ability not only to predict what would happen in the future but to influence or control it. And such an ability, of course, is 'beyond our understanding', the meaning we attribute to the word today.

WINE

The Ancient Greek word *oinos* has given almost every European language its word to describe the fermented juice of the grape. An even earlier Greek form of the word, *woinos*, is easily recognizable in such forms as English 'wine' (and, of course, 'vine'), Latin *vinum*, French *vin*, German *Wein*, Spanish and Italian *vino* and the Russian *vinó*. In slightly less recognizable forms the same root appears in Welsh *gwin* and Irish Gaelic *fion*.

The Indo-European root which produced all these forms is WI, 'to twist', 'to ramble' (seen also in the Latin infinitive *viere*, 'to weave together'), an obvious allusion to the way in which the vine naturally twists and turns as it grows. It is also cognate with the English word 'withy' as in the pub name 'The Withy Trees' where the adjective means nothing more than 'twisted'.

There is, however, an etymological footnote to the story of how the original *woinos* has influenced other languages. As we have seen, most modern European languages have preserved the Greek word in one form or another. In Modern Greek, however, the normal word for wine is *krasi*, and this has a pedigree no less fascinating than its earlier counterpart.

Homer's heroes, we are given to understand, would seldom, if ever, drink their wine neat. The usual custom was to mix it with water, and the Greek verb for this process of mixing or blending was *kerannumi*; the bowl in which the wine and water were mixed was called a *kratēr* (which gave us the word 'crater') and the process itself was known as *krasis*. So the Modern Greek for wine is, strictly speaking, 'a mixture'.

The Ancient Greeks had yet another word for 'wine', *methu*, although strictly speaking this could be applied to any strong drink and not just the product of the vine. It had found its way into Greek from Sanskrit, which had *mathu*, 'sweet', descriptive of any sweet drink in general and of honey in particular. Both words are the forebears of our 'mead'.

An unexpected linguistic cousin here is the word 'amethyst'. We now think of this word as being exclusively a term for a precious stone, but for the Ancient Greeks the word denoted a herb to which they attributed special qualities, in particular the ability to ward off drunkenness in mortals. Consequently the Modern Greek adjective *amethustos* means 'sober', 'not in an inebriated state'.

Perhaps the most interesting linguistic development here, however, is the connection with the Russian for 'bear', *medved*'. The first element of the word, *medv*, was originally *medu*, from the Sanskrit and Greek roots, and it eventually evolved into *myod*, the modern Russian for 'honey'. The second element, *-ed*, is a Slavonic root etymologically allied to the English verb 'to eat' and the adjective 'edible'. These elements combine in modern Russian to describe an animal that 'eats honey'.

Z

ZEAL

'Zeal' and its derivative adjective 'zealous' have come down to us via the Greek verb *zeō*, 'to boil', suggesting seething passion and heated devotion. This can also be seen in another Greek noun, *zēlōtēs*, 'zealot', which originally meant an admirer, imitator or follower of someone but which by New Testament times had acquired the stronger meaning of fervent devotee.

Another noun derived from the verb 'to boil' in Greek was *zema*, meaning 'that which has been boiled'. When prefixed with the word *eks*, 'out', a new word is formed: *ekszema* or, as it is now spelled in its English form, 'eczema'. In other words the skin complaint characterized by inflamed eruptions is really the Greek for 'that which has boiled out'.

The Indo-European root from which the Greek words are derived is YAS, 'to ferment', the recognizable base in words such as the adjective *zestos*, 'fervent', which later showed up in Anglo-Saxon as *gyst*, Middle English *yest* and the modern English word 'yeast'.

When we say that *zestos* means 'fervent' we are not so much translating the Greek word as using the Latin equivalent. *Fervere* is the Latin for 'to boil', and in addition to 'fervent' it has given us words such as 'ferment' and 'fervour'.

lexical links
at a glance

The following pages are intended as a rapid guide to the various headings and their associated words. It is hoped that such an 'in a nutshell' list will serve as an *aide-mémoire* for readers who have already familiarized themselves with the contents of the book, while at the same time it should be a useful guide for those who require a quick summary of the unlikely connections between many words in everyday usage.

a–c

ABACUS dust

ABSTEMIOUS choke – stifle

ACRE acorn

ACROBAT Acropolis – to egg on – to incite – to prick – to spur on – to snap – to crush – acidic – oxygen – vinegar – oxymoron – mediocre

AFTERMATH to reap – meadow

AKIMBO keen

AMBULANCE field hospital – clinic – to amble

ANATHEMA offering – curse

ANATOMY tome – to cut – section – sect – secateurs – sector – to gnaw – to nibble – to clip – to shear – tonsure – atom

ANGER anxiety – anguish – angst – angina – tonsillitis

ANTHOLOGY flower – posy – poesy – poem – verse – prose – stanza

ANTIQUE antic – eye – antler

APPETITE to attack – to contract – to starve – to die – thirst – dryness – torrid – terrace

APPLAUSE to clap hands – to explode – to go off

ARGUMENT bright – shining – glistening – swift-footed – silver – to shape – plastic – plasma – plaster

ASPHALT firmness – stability – security – to shake – seismograph – to tremble

ATLAS to bear – to suffer – to lift – to tolerate

ASYLUM seizure – reprisal – inviolate

ATHLETE prize – pledge – bride – to wed – to seize – to grab

AUCTION increase – Dutch auction

AUSPICIOUS favourable – divination – bird – flight – spectator – spectacle – scout – spy – sceptic

AUTHENTIC genuine –fake – murderer

BALD white – bald eagle – frost – fire – blaze

BANSHEE fairy

BARBARIAN foreigner – stammering – Slav – Slavonic – slave – speech – tale – German – dumb

BISTRO restaurant – quickly – snack bar

BLEMISH blue – to wound – to bruise – to break
BLESS to consecrate – blood – to sprinkle – to flower – to bloom – to flourish – blossom

BOG marsh – quagmire – soft

BOIL puss – bile – septic

BOMB buzzing – bumble bee – deodorant spray – fly spray – bulb – bomb-aimer – striker

BOTANY grass – pasture – fodder – proboscis

BOW AND ARROW to bend – bent – bowed – arc – arch – string – toxin – poison – potion – intoxicated – nerve – neuron – neurology – to go – venom – carry – drug – remedy – medicine – gullet – oesophagus – to eat

BRIDE to teem with – to be full – embryo

BRIDEGROOM ground – humility – humble – chameleon – lion

BROGUE shoe – accent

BUDDHA enlightened – to awaken – to become aware of – to enquire – alarm clock – beadle

CALAMITY destruction – hailstones – misfortune – to annoy – to trouble – to distress – plague – blow – disaster

CALCULATE pebble – stone – mathematics – to learn – astrologer – geometry – trigonometry – polygon – pentagon – hexagon – algebra – fragments

CALENDAR money-lender – calends

C

CALLOW youth – bare – beardless – naked

CANDIDATE to shine – toga – candle – candid – incandescent – white – tablet – album

CANOPY gnat – cone – optical – synopsis – myopia – autopsy

CARBUNCLE coal – charcoal – abscess – hearth – grate – grating – to weave – crass – dense – thick – curve – crate

CARDINAL to swing – hinge – pivot

CARNIVAL festivity – celebration – Lent – flesh – to cut off – carnation – holiday – banquet – lively – merry – bright

CAROL flute-player – dance – chorus – to blow – to pant – asthma – ravine – gully – channel – road – street – beehive

CARPENTER car – cart – furniture – cabinet-maker

CATACLYSM inundation – deluge – to wash over – to dash against –drain – sewer – cloacal

CATALOGUE military service – list – enlist

CATARACT waterfall – to crash down – gush – sluice – portcullis

CATASTROPHE to turn – dig – overturn

CATEGORY market – marketplace – to address – to declare – to accuse – to denounce – to signify – to intimate – to classify

CENTRE spike – goad – prick – boss – navel – umbilical

CHAMPION boxer – fighter – campus – warrior – struggle – to bend – curve – camera – chimney – chamber – oven – forge

CHEAP price –harbour – merchant – innkeeper – shopkeeper – to trade – to swindle – chop and change – chapman – chap – traveller – emporium – to tread – path – route – routine –commerce – mercantile – merchandise – wares – service – merit – to deal in – to traffic in – share

CHURCH kirk – lord – assembly – to summon – ecclesiastic – congregation – flock – cathedral – seat – to sit – chair – throne – chapel – shrine – synagogue – mosque – to adore – to prostrate oneself

CLERGY cleric – clerk – lot – portion – inheritance – to break off – to smash – fragment – priest – respected – honoured – revered – reverence – reverend – Presbyterian – Episcopal – vicar – deputy – curate – to care for – to attend – to cure

COLLEEN girl – uncle – granddad – man

CONFECTIONERY sweets – chocolate – to make – to prepare – tailor – the rag trade – off-the-peg

CONSIDER star – constellation – to meditate – to reflect upon

CONSTIPATION ship – trample – to pack together – to stiffen – stone – pebble – wall – to press – compacted – cold – influenza – to bind – to tie – strict – stricture – stringent

CONTEMPLATE temple – enclosure – survey – to cut off

COSMOS chaos – order – adornment – universe – world – galaxy – comet – coma – planet – to roam – to go astray – plankton – attendant – satellite – sputnik – fellow-traveller – path – way – meteor – star – layer – stratum – street – to sprinkle – straw – strewn

COSTERMONGER apple – monger – salesman – slave-trader – sleight of hand – to trick – to mingle – to mix – mongrel

COUP blow – box on the ears – to prune – to confine – to punish – to hew – to chisel – to peck – culpable – culprit

CRISIS judgement – decision – critical – to criticize – to judge – hypocrite – actor – pretender – underhand

c–f

CROCODILE lizard – pebble – gastric – gastrolith – gullet – mouth – womb

CUP vat – butt – hole – hollow – to bulge – hull – beehive – coop – heaven – ceiling

CUPID desire – love – hope – to boil – to breathe out – smoke – incense – vapour

CUSHION mattress – bolster – pillow – hipbone – armpit – knee joint

DAPPER neat – tidy – brave – steadfast – valiant

DEARTH scarcity – expensiveness

DECIDE to cut – precise – cement

DELICATE delightful – charming – milk – to wean

DELIRIUM insanity – furrow – track – footprint – last – to learn

DETECTIVE sleuth – to discover – to cover – to uncover – deck – roof – toga – togs – thatch – stegosaurus – covert – curfew – focus – hearth

DEVIL evil – to throw – ballistic – to slander – Satan – enemy – fiend –demon – genius – fate – fortune – to distribute – to allot – Lucifer – light – phosphorus – problem – parable – comparison – to speak – palaver – parliament

DIABETES to pass water – to urinate – to stand – compasses

DICE die – to move – to cross the Rubicon

DINNER hunger – fast – breakfast – lunch

DIPHTHERIA to soften – supple – to tan – leather

ELECTRICITY sun – to shine – to gleam – amber

ENORMOUS abnormal – norm – normal – irregular – unusual – mind – intelligence – gnome – gnomon – interpreter

ENOUGH to suffice – to reach – to obtain – to bring – to carry – bulk – burden

EXTRAVAGANT to wander – vague – to stray

FACULTY blind – deaf – dumb – confusion – to blend – to slumber – to blunder – dark – unseen – dim – Dublin

FAMILY servant – household – house

FANATIC fane – enthusiastic – profane – temple

FANTASTIC visible – display – to imagine – vision – image – dream

FARM to affirm – to settle – payment – grange – George – land

FATE to say – to ban – banns – to announce – to fascinate – to enchant – to bewitch – sorcerer – to attack verbally – to speak ill of – to put the evil eye on – to oppose – obstacle – destiny – to stand – share – portion – lot – to spin – to twist – to obtain by lots – to turn

FEE cattle – property – fief – feudal – to tie up – to bind – to fix – pact – page – peace – pecuniary – impecunious – peculiar – inexplicable – private – fellow

FICTION to shape – to form – to fashion – fact – to make – to do – to invent – to fabricate – to devise – falsehood – to lie – to break – to bend – to pretend

FINGER fang – to catch – five – thumb – tumult – tumulus – tumour – thimble – toe – digit – to take – to show – to teach

FIRE pyre – pyrotechnics – pyromania – Pyrex – pure – to purify – tinder – to ignite – bureau – office – borage – to stuff – to pad out – combustion – to burn

FISH Christianity – to save – saviour

FLEA flee – fly – flow – to jump – to stream – to sail – feather

FOLK folksy – crowd – army – infantry – rank and file – people – nation – regiment –

f–h

host – colonel – lieutenant-colonel – plethora – flock

FOOLHARDY fool – to make bold – hard – power – strength – democracy – aristocracy – plutocracy

FOREST woodland – abroad – outside – park – paddock – to enclose – to fence off – to fasten – bar – spar – spear

FRIEND lover – to love – wife – Friday

FRUIT produce – enjoyment – to have the benefit of – to make use of – to need

GALE furious – to enchant

GARGOYLE throat – waterspout – gullet – windpipe – eddy – whirlpool – to gurgle – to gargle – Gargantua

GAZETTE magpie – journal – news – periodical – daily – ephemeral – chronicle – echo – annals – catechism – grasshopper – magazine – storehouse

GLASNOST voice – town – garden – castle – cock – to call

GLAUCOMA owl – coals to Newcastle – bright – gleaming – shining – to laugh – pupil – neat – small – careful – clean – sticky – clammy – oily – clay – glue – sleek – lard – tallow – vegetable oil

GO Andalucía – Vandals – to wander – went

GOB beak – gift of the gab – cheek – jowl – neck

GOSSIP sponsor – godparent – godfather – sibling – kinsman

GRAVE to dig – to engrave – to write – to carve – hieroglyph – coffin – basket – tomb – mausoleum – sarcophagus – cemetery – bed

GROG rum – cloak – cloth

GROTESQUE cave – grotto – crypt – to hide – cryptic – Apocrypha

HALCYON kingfisher – solstice – sea – to conceive – pregnant – cyst – crater – casserole

HALO to roll – voluble – volume – wallet – wallow

HANDCUFFS fetter – wife

HARANGUE ring – market

HARBOUR refuge – army – shelter – room – lodgings – hostel – harbinger – borough – burrow – burglar – robber – to harry – to ravage – to lay waste – haven

HARPOON to grasp – to seize – rapacious – prey – hook – robbery – seizure – rape – cramp-iron – rake – harrow – hearse – to rehearse – sharp – sickle – scythe – to cut – scorpion – Harpies

HEART to quiver – to throb – cardiac – cordial

HELL eternity – damnation – torment – to hide – to cover – helmet – hall – cell – cellar – conceal – eucalyptus – Hades – underworld – Pluto – rich – inferior

HIPPOPOTAMUS river – horse – equine – equestrian – quick – runner – swift – cavalier – cavalry – cavalcade – dromedary – palfrey – hunter – to pull – marshal – mare – constable – stable – potable – to feed – to nourish – to protect – to drink – stream – pot – pasture – pastor – repast – bread – to bake – food – to feed – powerful – lord – possessor – husband – spouse – father – master – guest – host – xenophobia – stranger – foreigner – enemy – hostile – host – hospital – hotel – hostel despot – tyrant

HORMONE attack – instinct – to stir up – to rouse – to excite – to rise up – to orientate – to leap – to dance – orchestra – bird – ornithologists – origin

HUBRIS pride – violence – aggression – riotousness – assault – battery – Nemesis – to be displeased with – hybrid

HUSSAR corsair – plunderer

HYGIENE cleanliness – health – sanitation – unsanitary – fit – sane – vigorous – strong – vegetable – vegetation – to wax

HYPOCHONDRIAC porridge – gruel – corn – grain

h–n

– groats – cartilage

IDEA to see – vision – video – to know – Vedas – wit – witch

INK to burn – calm

JUBILEE sabbatical – ram – ram's horn

JUGGLER acrobat – magician – joke – joker – jester – to do – to perform – buffoon – fool – to puff up – bouffant – windbag – troubadours – to find – to compose – minstrel – beggar – crook – rascal – truant – idler – loafer

KISS to taste – to choose

LADY loaf – to knead – to mould – dough – lord – dyke – wall – paradise – Eden – delight – to enjoy oneself – sty – steward – to arrange – to march – rank of soldiers – line of poetry – verse

LEPRECHAUN fairy – sprite – small – body

LETHARGIC Lethe – drowsy – sleepy – to quit – to leave – to remain hidden – to go unnoticed – to forget – latent – work – lethal – death

LIBIDO to desire – to love – to please – wilful – passionate – free

LIBRARY book – bookshop – bark – paper – beech – lobby – foliage – leaf – bower – bast – pulp fiction – leprosy – peel

– to put – granary – store – chemist's – apothecary – to pour – wine store – gallery – to amuse oneself – pilgrimage

LICHGATE/LYCHGATE churchyard – coffin – corpse – like – kingly – manly – earthly

LINGER long – to slacken – to make loose – slow – laggard – to be faint – to be weak – languid – to languish – to long for

LUCRE profit – gain – plunder – booty – price – wages – reward – to attempt to catch – to acquire as spoil

MACHINE device – contrivance – to construct – machinations – to have power – to be able – might – may – main

MAFIA to brag – to strut – Matthew – tax-collector

MAWKISH sentimentality – insipidness – maggot – moth – worm – insect – to chew – mandible – masticate

MEAT to measure – fat – to be wet – to drip – mastoid – breast – Amazon – mastodon

MERRY pleasant – joyful – short – brief – to shrink – to wither – ardour – mirth – sportive

METAL mine – quarry – in search of – to follow – mineral – to dig

METICULOUS fear –

apprehension – dread – coward

MEWS cage – to moult – to change

MIGRATE immigrate – emigrate – to change place – to change – exchange – recompense – repayment – barter – alteration – amoeba – metabolism

MOB to move – to push

MONEY Juno – mint – to advise – to warn – to admonish – monster – mind – mentality – scales – to weigh – to think – pensive – solid – soldier – cash – denier – handful – to grasp – dollar – mark – penny – pawn – pledge – shilling – to divide – to cut – lance – axe – cleaver

MOON month – to measure – selenology – lunatic

MUCUS discharge – to wipe – nostril – nozzle – wick – fuse – match – snot – snuff – snout – to sniff – candle

MURDER death – dead – to die – desert – sea – mere – marsh – swamp – sump – pond – porous

MYSTERY to shut – to bite one's lips – to keep mum

NARCISSUS narcissism – narcotic – drowsiness – stupor – contractions – cramp – to twist – to entwine – to grow numb – numbness – torpedo

NEIGHBOUR nigh – near –

n–p

tiller – dweller – to grow – to build – to dwell – to be – boor – farmer – bower – arbour – husband – husbandman – to manage

NIB bill – beak – Thoth – scribe – ibis

NICE subtle – stupid – to know – science – knowledge

NIGHT dead – lost – invisible – to perish – sleep

NIGHTMARE weight – incubus – to lie heavily – to incubate – dream

NOMAD pasture – to dwell – to hold – to deal out – Nemesis – to distribute

NOON midday – ninth hour

NYMPH bride – to marry – to cover – nubile – cloud – sky – rocks

OBITUARY funeral rite – death – downfall – setting – to go to meet

ODD triangle – spear – place

ODEON song – poem – poetry – rhapsody – recitation – lyric – to sew – to stitch

OFFAL meat – entrails – garbage – rubbish

OSTRACIZE blackballing – potsherd – oyster – bone – shell – osteoarthritis – osteoporosis

PANIC fear – Pan – Dionysus – festival

PANTRY bread – company – to accompany – larder – fat – lard – sweet – tasty

PARASITE corn – grain – food – guest – toady – to flatter

PAWNBROKER pledge – security – deposit – lumber

PAY peace – to placate – to appease – remuneration – gift – reward – stipend – tax – contribution – emolument – miller – mill – to grind – effort – gain – advantage – molar – salary – wages – salt

PERIOD way – road – journey – to travel – chart – map – orbit – method – exodus – anode – cathode – diode – to go – itinerary – itinerant – ambient – ambition – year – isthmus – step – movement

PETARD trap – bomb – to break wind – to fart – banger

PETITION to make for – to head for – to attack – to assail – to strive for – to seek to attain – to fetch – to derive – to ask for – to beg – to beseech – to request – impetus – to fly – feather – wing – pen

PHALANX block of wood – tree trunk – log – penis – wooden – pale – pole

PLAGIARIZE kidnapper – net – stealing – to move

sideways – slanting – at an angle – treacherous – underhand

POLICY police – politics – town – fold – to fold up – to show – to demonstrate – diploma – twice – diplomat

POLLEN flour – meal – to brandish – to swing – to toss

PORNOGRAPHY prostitute – to write – to draw – to sell oneself – harlot – to sell for export or slavery – vault – arch – brothel – to fornicate

PORT AND STARBOARD left-hand side – larboard – rudder – to steer

PRECARIOUS unsafe – unsure – prayer – to pray – to ask

PREVARICATE double-crossing – bent – knock-kneed – crooked – straddling – varicose veins

PSALM to touch – plectrum – to strike – to stroke – finger – hand – to feel – to fumble

PSYCHIATRIST psychologist – mind – soul – to blow – to breathe – to draw breath – to breathe – doctor – healer – to heal – to cure – to warm – to cheer – to move – to be vigorous – warmth – hot-blooded – wrath – ire – gadfly – oestrus – oestrogen

PUDDING sausage – paunch – bag – to swell – intestines – entrails

p-s

PUMPKIN melon – ripe – to cook – to boil – to bake – to digest – peptic – dyspepsia – indigestion

PYTHON snake – serpent – Delphic oracle – pythoness – witch – sorceress – female seer – to destroy – to slay

QUAFF cup – goblet – carouse – to booze – boozer – pipe – tube – tap

READY to ride – to go on a raid – road

REEK smoke – smell – vapour – belch – vomit – eructation – to burn – to smoulder – cloud – dust – typhus

RELUCTANT unwilling – to wrestle – pliable – flexible – to bend – to twist – to throw – lock

REVEAL cloth – veil – to draw back – sail – to pull – vehicle

RISK rock-face – to cut – cliff

RIVER bank – shore – riparian – arrive

ROBOT labour – slave – work – orphan – heir – inheritance

RODENT to gnaw – corrode – erode – rostrum – beak – snout – prow – to scratch – rat – mouse – to steal – muscle – mole

ROYAL regal – regent – to rule – reign – right – rajah – bishopric – to reach – to stretch – anger – passion – to swell – orgasm – rich

RUBBISH/RUBBLE to reave – to steal – to plunder – to rob – robe

SABOTAGE clog – inefficiency – to mess up – to botch

SACK bag – sieve – strainer – beard – to give the sack – skittles – bag and baggage – ransack

SARDONIC scornful – sneering

SCANDAL trap – to trip up – bait

SCAVENGER to look at – to display – rubbish

SCHOOL leisure – spare time – academy – lyceum – wolf – prostitute – college – guild – society – colleague – university – universe – union – gymnasium – grammar school – comprehensive – to grasp – to include – prison – technology – art – skill – to join together – tutor – to fasten – to construct – implement – artillery piece – lecture – lesson – to read – seminar – seedbed – tutor – tutorial – to protect – professor – to avow – busy – zealous – class – pupil – orphan – teacher – to show – doctor – docile

SCONE pancake – bread – bright – beautiful – sheen

SEASON spring – seed – crops – to release – to let fly – to cast – to sow – to scatter – semen – to sprinkle – sporadic – spore – sperm – sparse – diaspora – enema – time – to cut – early – summer – to light up – to kindle – to heat up – thermos – thermometer – autumn – harvest – to grow – happy – rich – prosperous – fall – winter – rain-water – otter – cold – frost – snow – to pour

SEDUCE to lead away – to lead astray – secure – sedition – separate – to set apart

SHAMBLES slaughterhouse – bench – to support – to prop up – sceptre

SHARK sharp-pointed – jagged – to shirk – loiter – prowl

SHILLELAGH cudgel – oak – blackthorn – willow – leash – thong

SHINGLES rash – midriff – belt – to surround – herpes – to creep – to crawl – serpent

SHOP stall – booth – cowshed – shippon – cover – to shield – shade – shadow – squirrel – squire

SHOPLIFTER to steal – thief – rogue – kleptomania

SHROVETIDE time – shrift – Lent – penance – to write – punishment

s-t

SINCERE pure – uncontaminated – wax – genuineness – honesty – mix – destruction – decay – to smash – to destroy – strife – din – slain – to choose

SKETCH near – sudden – spur of the moment – extempore speech

SLOGAN public – crowd – host – army – flock – call – mobilization – catchphrase

SMASHING good – beautiful

SOAP fat – grease – wool – sheep – ewe – lanolin – pet – devoted to – attached to – pleased – satisfied

SOOTHSAYER sooth – to be – to soothe – to assuage – to calm

SPOON chip – shaving – wedge – kindling – spade

SPORT disport – to amuse – to play – to carry

STIGMA marked – branded – to prick – to pierce – to thrust – to smite –stick – stake – sting – to roast – steak – character

STIRRUP to climb – rope – stile – rising – sty – barleycorn – staff – crozier – saltire – to leap – to spring

STRATEGY stratagem – general – army – universal – tactical – position – arrangement – to place

SUDDEN under – stealthily – unseen – underhand – to approach

SURGEON manual labour – hand – work – surgery – foot – chiropodist – manoeuvre – manure – to till

SWASTIKA well-being – fortune – fylfot – gammadion

SYCOPHANT litigant – fig

TALK sense – to interpret – to explain

TANTALIZE Tantalus

TARIFF notification – knowledge

TATTOO drawing – tap – taproom

TAVERN hut – shop – booth – beam – timber – tent – tabernacle

TAWDRY cheap and cheerful – gaudy – showy – ornament – celebration – to rejoice – joy – to enjoy – jewel

TAXI to measure – to touch – to handle – to weigh – to estimate

TENTERHOOKS tapestry – tenter – to stretch – tent – to draw – tone – tense – to tend – thin – to elongate – antenna

THEATRE to behold – to see – to gaze – amphitheatre – drama – to do – effective – drastic – tragedy – goat – comedy – revelry – merry-

making – village – to lull – to put to sleep – cemetery

THERAPY to worship – to flatter – to pay court to – to cultivate – pay attention to – servant – slave

THRESHOLD to thresh – to thrash – to snap – to crackle – to pop – wood – forest – weald

THROMBOSIS to nourish – to rear – curdled – milk – cheese – clot

TIME tide – hour – to happen – tidings – tidy – neat

TOILET dressing – gown – cloth – to weave – texture – text – subtle –web – to tidy up – to clean up – necessary

TOY tool – implement – book – plaything – utensil

TRAVEL work – travail – rod

TREACLE antidote – animal compounds – venomous – deer – wilderness – soul – bewilder

TREE oak – dryad – rhododendron – druid – health – durable – strong – trim – robust

TRIUMPH victory – hymn – merriment – rejoicing

TRIVIAL crossroads – ordinary – commonplace – geometry – music –arithmetic – astronomy – grammar – rhetoric – logic – to rub – road

t–z

TROGLODYTE cave-dweller – hole – to gnaw – diver – to plunge – nibbler – trout

TROPHY triumph – to turn – sword – helmet

TRY to attempt – to test – to rub – to select – to sift – to spend time – pastime – discussion – argument – diatribe – attrition – detriment – detritus – trite – tribulation

UMBRELLA parasol – sun – shadow – shade – rain – water – protection

USHER door – mouth – oral – kiss – osculating

VACCINATE cowpox – smallpox – cow – to cry – to low – vocal – voice – eye – to see – bud – to graft on to – to implant

VETERINARY (SURGEON) beast of burden – old – year – veteran

VIOLIN fiddle – calf – heifer – veal

VIRUS slime – liquid – venom – poison – to melt – to liquefy – birdlime – mistletoe – viscous – viscosity – twig – to sprinkle – dung – manure – fog – mist – gloom – to pass water – micturition – urine

WACK son – Scousers – Gaelic – warrior – follower – lobscouse – stew – sloppy – mushy

WAR confusion – to perplex – to limp – to come to ruin – to perish – chaos – to travel – to twist – to turn – furrow – furlong – worse – complicated

WASSAIL whole – hale – hello – beautiful

WEAPON panoply – equipment – implement of war – armour – hoplite – to prepare – to train

WEIRD strange – mysterious – inexplicable – destiny – to become

WINE vine – to twist – to ramble – to weave – withy – mixture – sweet – honey – mead – amethyst – sober – to eat – edible – bear

ZEAL to boil – zealot – devotee – eczema – to ferment – yeast – fervour

bibliography

dictionaries

Atkins, Beryl T., Alain Duval, Rosemary C. Milne (eds), *The Collins Robert French Dictionary*, HarperCollins, London,1990

Ayto, J., *Dictionary of Word Origins*, Bloomsbury, London, 1990

de Bhaldraithe, T. (ed.), *English–Irish Dictionary*, Oifig an tSoláthair, Dublin, 1959

Diccionario de la Lengua Española, Real Academia Española, Madrid, 1992

Dinneen, P.S., *Foclóir Gaedhilge agus Béarla (An Irish–English Dictionary)*, Irish Texts Society, Dublin, 1927

Hoad, T.F. (ed.), *The Oxford Concise Dictionary of English Etymology*, Oxford University Press, Oxford, 1996 (revised version of the *Oxford Dictionary of English Etymology* compiled by C.T. Onions, G.W.S. Friedrichsen and R.W. Burchfield, 1966)

Istorichesko-etimologicheskiy slovar' sovremennogo russkogo yazyka (Historical Etymological Dictionary of Modern Russian), Russkiy Yazyk, Moscow, 2001

Jarman, B., G. and R. Russell (eds), *The Oxford Spanish Dictionary*, Oxford University Press, Oxford, 1994

Liddel and Scott's Greek–English Lexicon, Clarendon Press, Oxford, 1864 and 1963 editions

Simpson, D.P., *Latin–English/English–Latin Dictionary*, Cassell, 1959

Skeat, W., *A Concise Etymological Dictionary of the English Language*, Clarendon Press, Oxford, 1956; also Wordsworth edition, 1993

Terrell, P. (ed.), *The Oxford German Dictionary*, Oxford University Press, Oxford, 1990

Wade, T., *Russian Etymological Dictionary*, University of Bristol, Bristol, 1996

Wheeler. M., and B. Unbegaun (eds), updated by Colin Howlett, *The Oxford Russian Dictionary*, Oxford University Press, Oxford, 1993

Wyld, H.C. (ed.), *The Universal Dictionary of the English Language*, Herbert Joseph, London, 1932

other works consulted

Blakely, L ., *Old English*, English Universities Press, London, 1973

Crystal, D., *The Cambridge Encyclopedia of Language*, Cambridge University Press, Cambridge, 1995

Evslin, B., *Gods, Demigods and Demons*, Scholastic Book Services, New York, 1975

Giles, P., *A Short Manual of Comparative Philology*, Macmillan, London, 1901

Jónsson, S., *A Primer of Modern Icelandic*, Oxford University Press, Oxford, 1972

Matthews, W., *Russian Historical Grammar*, Athlone Press, London, 1960

Mavromataki, M., *Greek Mythology and Religion*, Haitalis, Athens, 1997

Miles, E., *How to Learn Philology*, Swan Sonnenschein and Co., London and New York, 1899

Pei, M., *The Story of Language*, Allen and Unwin, London, 1968

Rose, H., *Gods and Heroes of the Greeks,* New English Library, London, 1974

Smith, F.K., *Latin,* English Universities Press, London, 1964

Thomson, G., *The Greek Language*, Heffer and Sons, Cambridge, 1960